How to Effecti

Manage

Who is to blame for the 2008 fir

- The bankers who are accused of recklessly gambling with people's money?
- The lenders who accepted the loans when they knew they could not afford the repayment?
- The politicians who failed to regulate the financial system?
- Dick Fuld, the former boss of Lehman Brothers who let his bank go down?
- Henry Paulson, Secretary of the Treasury of the United States who refused to bail out Lehman Brothers?
- The British government that refused to approve the Barclays deal?
- The market that devalued the banks stock?

I could go on and on and the list will continue to get longer and we might still not arrive at the real culprit.

As I was completing the final edit of this book, I took a break to watch the news. A program called Meltdown was on Al Jazeera English channel. It was a documentary about how the 2008 financial crisis came into being.

In the documentary they showed extracts of interviews with those who were in key positions at the time. What was interesting about the interviews was that, not a single person took responsibility for their involvement in the financial collapse. Without exception every single one of them pointed the blame at someone or something else.

As I listened to them, I came to the conclusion that failure to take responsibility and identify the root course of the 2008 financial collapse is the reason why just two years later, we find ourselves in another financial crisis.

What does the financial crisis have to do with you making 7 Figure in your law firm?

Maybe nothing!

Then again it might be everything!

Why are you currently not making 7 Figure per annum in your law firm?

Let me guess:

- You are unable to attract new clients
- You are having difficulties retaining existing clients
- Clients are not paying their bills
- Et cetera, et cetera, et cetera.

Has it occurred to you that you might not be attracting new clients because your marketing strategy is wrong?

You may be having difficulties retaining existing clients because your customer service leaves a lot to be desired?

Your clients might not be paying their bills because your pricing structure is wrong? Have you ever thought in that manner?

I guess not, otherwise you will already be making 7 Figure per annum.

In the last few years, thousands of law firms have been forced to shut down or be bought over by larger law firms.

The entrepreneur lawyers who sold out placed the blame for their demise on the economic crisis.

As I write one of the biggest law firms in the world has just declared bankruptcy, blaming difficult trading conditions for its demise.

While some entrepreneur lawyers are closing shops and blaming their woes on the economic crisis, others are racking in millions.

So what is the difference?

That is what this book is about…

The business of law is a lucrative business because at some point everyone gets into legal wrangle. We now live in a lawsuit century where people get sued for simple mistakes.

No law firm should struggle to make 7 Figure per annum in this lawsuit century let alone go bust.

It is possible for your law firm to make 7 Figure per annum guaranteed. Do you want to know how?

The how is in the book you are holding in your hands right now (You have on your screen).

Business success is a formula. Every successful business has used the identical formula to succeed.

Every business has a hundred per cent chance of succeeding and a hundred per cent chance of failing. It all depends on five core fundaments. Those fundamentals can be found in the book you are holding (You have on your screen).

There are law firms that are making 7 Figure per annum, learn how they are doing it. It is all inside the 7 Figure Code.

You are struggling to make 7 Figure per annum because like those guys in the documentary, you are blaming instead of fixing the problem. At the end of this book, you will know how to fix your problem, it is my promise and guarantee to you.

About the Author

Romeo Richards is the founder of the Business Education Centre, an institute that shows professional entrepreneurs such as doctors, lawyers, dentists, consultants, trainers, coaches, and security firm owners how to make "7 Figure" in twelve months. He is also the creator of the Business Success Quadrangle Framework and The Blue Ocean Strategy Canvas for: doctors, lawyers, dentists, consultants, retailers, coaches, trainers and security firms.

He has authored eight books on retail profit improvement and is currently writing four additional books on retail store design, visual merchandising, how to market a retail store and how to make profit in retail and the "How to effectively market and manage a profes-sional firm" series for doctors, lawyers, dentists, consultants, trainers, coaches and security firms.

He has authored several White Papers and regularly writes articles on entrepreneur development, retail profit improvement and speak on the same.

How to Effectively Market and Manage a Law Firm

Romeo Richards

www.theprofitexperts.co.uk

+44(0)78 650 49508

romeo@theprofitexperts.co.uk

Dedication

I wrote about vision as your reason for doing anything. I do what I do first and foremost to be an example to my son.

Secondly, to have the ability to help my people shed the curse of poverty.

Alex this book is for you!

Africa this book is in your honour!

Table of Contents

Acknowledgements

My sincere gratitude to Mr. White, John and Michael for editing the book.

Thanks Jen for formatting it and Joseph for managing the entire project.

How to Effectively Market and Manage a Law Firm

Romeo Richards

www.theprofitexperts.co.uk

+44(0)78 650 49508

romeo@theprofitexperts.co.uk

Why You Should Read This Book

Let me tell you a story.

In his E-Myth series, author Michael Gerber wrote that every business is a family business. At the time I read it, I did not understand what he meant until I had a business failure which resulted in the breakup of my own family.

However, please don't shed tears for me; you need to understand that despite my own painful circumstances, business success can be gratifying. There is no better feeling than realising your ambition and making a difference in the lives of others. I have a long list of former employees who otherwise would have been condemned to cleaning for the rest of their lives, because of me, they were able to pay their university tuition fees and are government officials in their native countries.

For decades the world has struggled to find a malaria vaccine for the developing world. With the financial and personal support of the Gates foundation, we are one step closer to eradicating this preventable illness. HIV was ravaging large areas of Africa at one point threatening to decimate the entire population of Southern Africa. Bill Gates made one of those life affirming decisions, he left Microsoft and got personally involved with his foundation. As a result of his personal involvement, the high rates of HIV infection in Africa are at last showing signs of slowing down and becoming manageable.

Why have I chosen to illuminate my own personal story and the achievements of Bill Gates?

When any business fails there are consequences, both positive and negative. Like me you could lose your love ones, your house, your car and everything you have worked hard for. Believe me those debt collectors don't joke when they show up at your door, even your cat is not immune.

However, when you succeed, there are no words in the dictionary that can describe the feelings of elation and joy that owning a successful business can bring. It's not just about the money. The money is great because you can now take those vacations you have been dreaming of. For me the sense of making a difference in the lives of others supersedes all other personal attainments. In this same sense I think we can all agree that preventing entire communities from being wiped from the face of the earth is more gratifying to Mr Gates than his 50 billion dollars.

Every business has a 100% chance of succeeding or a 100% chance of failing. Whichever way the scale tips depends upon four plus one key fundamentals:

- Visionary leadership
- "A" level people
- Robust system
- Effective marketing system
- Good business model

I started my business in 2004, by 2006 I was making £500,000 per annum which at the time was a million USD. By 2008 the worm had turned and I was £200,000 in debt. How and why did this happen to me? How did this refugee from Africa who arrived with just his ambition had it all and then lose it virtually overnight.

Like most people who start out in business I believed that business is common sense. On my own personal "road to Damascus" I was to learn that business is more than just a good idea and anything but common sense.

As I took stock and sought answers to why I fell from grace, it slowly dawned on me that if we don't prepare for success then we are preparing ourselves for failure. What do I mean by this?

As I write this preface, Facebook is about to be floated for approximately $95 billion. Facebook is just eight years old, what is it that makes Facebook so successful as a business? Bear in mind that before Facebook there were other social media sites.

Google has become synonymous with search engines and internet optimisation. But before Google, there were other search engines. So what did Google get right that other search engine providers got wrong?

Apple is today the most valuable company in the world, even more valuable than the US government. In the first quarter of 2012 Apple made a profit of US$11.6 billion, that's more profit than some Plcs. annual turnover.

So what do Facebook, Apple, Google and the rest of the other successful companies around the world have to do with you?

Everything!

The founders of Facebook, Google or Apple were just like you. Like you and I, they made the decision to establish a business. But they succeeded beyond even their own wildest imaginations. Why did they achieve the level of success that they did?

Even though Gates and Steve Jobs are academically bright they understood this simple yet profound fact, business is not common sense. To succeed in business like in any other profession requires certain skill sets.

The gap between one thousand pounds and a million pound is just a single idea or getting a single decision right.

Contained within this book is a formula that would help you make the right decisions for your business. Every successful business or entrepreneur has used this identical formula to succeed.

It was announced in May 2012 that the UK was officially in recession. All over the news there were images of shop closures, members of the public, business leaders and government officials commenting on how difficult this year was going to be. The world economy was failing, France and Greece were adding fire to the Eurozone crisis, the press were tainted with allegations of "phone hacking", what a year.

Meanwhile in the first quarter of 2012, Apple made sales of US$39.2 billion. The tabloids did not write about this because bad news is easier to sell.

So before you begin to say that the founders of Facebook, Google, Apple or the other successful businesses where lucky, let's put to bed a commonly held belief in business or life in general; there is no such thing as luck, it's an abstract concept that infers outside forces are responsible for success or failure. When you are prepared physically and mentally to take advantage of the opportunities that come your way, that's when you make your own luck.

I've previously mentioned that there are four plus one elements to running a successful business. The fifth and some would say the most contentious element is a good business model.

Your business model is the most critical element in the success or failure of your business. I made the point earlier that before Facebook, there were other social media sites. Before Google, there were other search engines. So what did Facebook and Google get right that the others got so wrong? Quite simply they developed a better business model.

There are lots of business books out there written by super successful entrepreneurs, so why is my book any different? What can I teach you that hasn't been taught by those ultra-successful entrepreneurs?

There are four main types of business books:

- Celebrity endorsement
- Highly researched and informative
- Me too
- Effective strategies

Celebrity endorsement:

Celebrity endorsed business books are those written by celebrity entrepreneurs such as Donald Trump, Richard Branson, Alan Sugar, Robert Kiyosaki etc.

These books can be subdivided into:

- Written by the celebrity before they became successful. No one knew the author at the time, therefore, the books included great contents.
- Now successful in their area of expertise these books contain all the usual I did it so you can do it mumbo-jumbo, completely removed from reality.
- Penned by a clever author who understands the power of a name. In most instances the celebrity never takes the time to read the manuscript.

Highly researched and informative:

Written mainly by academics or business journalists; based upon solid research. They are usually well written in academic or journalistic style and language. The only problem with these books is their level of complexity for the average reader. Even when you reread them and eventually understand the principles, implementing the information into your business can be difficult.

Me too:

Me too business books are written by wannabe experts, who write books just to be able to say they have published a book. In most cases these books contain no real substances and do not reveal any new insights into their so-called expertise.

Effective strategies:

Templates with a purpose of providing information and showing readers how to implement those changes into their businesses. Like the highly researched information books, they provide effective content. Unlike the highly researched research books, Effective strategy books help their readers implement their theories and ideas.

What differentiates this book from other business books is that it belongs to the forth category. It actually teaches you how to do what is written in the book.

At the end of this book you will learn the four plus one fundamentals that are responsible for a successful business. You will also have a step by step guide of how to implement those changes into your business.

Every Monday and Thursday I pick my son up from school. I once told my assistant that going to pick him up was like "going on a date with a beautiful woman". He reignites my fire to succeed every time I see him. Unfortunately I don't live with my son and I have to return him to his mother at the end of our time together. The agony and pain I feel as I drive away is unimaginable.

If your business fails, it can have unintended consequences on the ones you love. Don't you owe it to them to gain the requisite knowledge to at least give it your best shot?

This book will provide you the information you need to succeed in your business. It is your instruction manual to effectively market and manage your firm.

Introduction

This is a self-help instruction manual on how to make '7 Figures' per annum as an entrepreneur lawyer. Since I developed this concept the question that I am asked time and time again is "why are you so certain that I can make a 7 Figure within a year"?

I explain that with my formula their chances of success will increase by at least 100%. It is based on the same formula that has been used by all successful businesses since the beginning of trade and commerce in the modern world.

We all know the formula (H20) equals water, Newton's laws of motion have been established for almost three centuries and they remain true to this day. No one has yet to disprove Einstein's Theory of Relativity, his theories are as relevant today as they were years ago when Einstein first theorised them.

This book is about the timeless principles of business success. It's the same principles that allowed Facebook to float for $104 billion after only eight years of existence. It's the same principles that made Google synonymous with search engines even though there were several high profile search engines on the net. Microsoft's Bill Gates used these principles to build a business from nothing and become the richest man on the planet. It's the same principles that will turn your law firm into a success story.

Chapter one:

The first chapter of this book deals with the business fundamentals: the 'four plus one' business fundamentals that are critical for success. As an entrepreneur lawyer your first action must be to create a clear vision of what your firm will eventually look like when it is finally matured.

To help you achieve this vision you need:

- The right people: the right 'A' level people can accelerate the speed and level of your business success. Without them your job is made harder.
- Robust systems: without a robust operational system firmly embedded throughout your firm, the daily operations will be chaotic resulting in client dissatisfaction.
- Effective marketing strategy: no business can succeed without attracting new customers. To attract the various categories of clients your firm needs, will require an effective marketing strategy.

We'll show you how to create your vision, recruit the right people and how to create a robust administrative and marketing system for your firm.

Chapter two:

Further expands on the marketing strategy by providing a step by step guide on how to effectively market your law firm.

Chapter three:

How do you create a new market for your firm? With the internet breaking the monopolisation of the factors of distribution, providing consumers with infinite choices, law firms are witnessing their clients numbers dwindle. However, 90% of the clients currently using the services of law firms are unhappy with their current legal service providers. This opens an opportunity for you to attract their attention. But how can you go about this in an ethical way? This chapter shows you how to do that.

Chapter four:

Outlines the most effective strategies for recruiting and retaining 'A talents' for your firm. Bill Gates once said "Take away our best 20 people and Microsoft would become an unimportant company." Bear in mind Microsoft has close to half a million employees and yet Mr Gates believes that taking away just 20 'A' level people would make the company irrelevant. This is the power of having the right people within your organisation. This chapter shows you how to recruit and retain 'A talents' in your firm.

Chapter Five:

Dive into the most important aspect of the life of an entrepreneur lawyer. Entrepreneur lawyers like most entrepreneurs put in the hours. While this is necessary to ensure your success, it also reduces your productivity. It is not the amount of hours you put in that matters but how 'smart' you have worked. Remember it is productivity that counts not activities. Chapter five shows you how to increase your productivity tenfold without increasing your activities and number of working hours.

Chapter six:

How do you know that your office assistant is not spending half his working day on Facebook? How do you know when your clients are dissatisfied with your services? How do you know if your marketing resources are being allocated effectively? Chapter six contain the systems and tools necessary for measuring your own performance and the performance of each and every member of your team.

Chapter seven:

What's holding you back from expansion? What's the simplest way of achieving your vision? My simplified version of the "Theory of Constraint" (TOC) can be used to diagnose your current level of success and plot the most appropriate course for achieving your goals. This is what chapter seven teaches you.

Chapter eight:

Becoming a partner within a law firm is what most junior lawyers aspire to. The road to partnership is not paved with gold. For most junior lawyers, it can be a long and tedious process, however, through hard work, patience and a lot of ambition the journey can be financially beneficial. Chapter eight outlines the steps necessary to make partnership successful within any law firm.

Chapter nine:

This final chapter deals with change. Change is the only thing that is constant. With the internet and the level of change taking place in every industry, you cannot continue doing things the old ways and expect to succeed. Change will come whether you like it or not. Are you prepared to be a master or victim of change? Illustrating the transformation strategies employed by the U.S. Army to transform itself from a Cold War army to one fit for the 21st century, I outlined various steps that you can take to prepare your law firm for the changing world.

Chapter ten:

One chronic malady afflicting many law firms is the lack of succession planning. Succession planning refers to the intended activities, processes and programs put in place by a law firm to guarantee a smooth transfer of responsibilities and leadership to a succeeding generation of lawyers and managers.

Essential to the success and long term endurance of law firms are a well mapped out succession planning that immediately takes effect and maintain the firm's competitive advantage in the marketplace. In chapter ten I will outline the importance of succession planning and lay down precise step by step instructions on how to develop a plan for your law firm.

Every business needs the services of a lawyer, yet lawyers struggle to make 7 Figure per annum. It should not be that way. There are a lot of tools at your disposal that can make it possible for you to achieve a 7 Figure revenue per annum. Outlined in each chapter of this book are those tools and ways of taking advantage of them.

Chapter One: How to Make 7 Figures Annually as an Entrepreneur Lawyer

The legal profession is facing one of its biggest challenges yet since the beginning of the profession. There are several changes taking place within the profession that would affect the way the business of law is conducted:

- There was the introduction of the "Tesco law" and the 'outcomes focused' regulations in October of 2011.
- The renewal of the profession indemnity insurance, which removes the collective cover of law firms resulting in many law firms obtaining the "Assigned Risks Pool" status.
- The housing bubble bust almost completely wiping out the conveyancing sector forcing many law firms to change their salary structure to "eat what you kill".
- Client becoming move savvy with the internet making it easy to find legal advice online
- Large business opening their own internal legal departments to reduce legal cost

These are in addition to operational challenges such as:

- Attracting new clients
- Retaining existing clients
- Attracting and retention "A talents"
- The Jackson Reforms

As I edit this chapter, Dewey & LeBoeuf one of the biggest law firms in the world has filed for chapter 11 bankruptcy protection. The main reason given for its demise is the economic slowdown which reduced its revenue stream making it difficult for the firm to meet its obligations to its partners.

The question that is on everyone's mind is for whom will the bell tolls next?

Dewey & LeBoeuf like most failing law firms, blame their demise on the economy. Some other struggling law firms would blame a second culprit: the new regulations.

But are law firms struggling or failing because of the economic crisis or the new regulations?

There is no doubt that the economic crisis has affected a lot of businesses. The introduction of new regulations in any industry is bound to have an adverse effect on some businesses within the industry.

However, can the economic crisis and the introduction of new legal regulations be considered the core problem affecting the legal profession?

I believe the answer to the above question is no.

It is true that an economic slowdown would affect certain industries more than others. As consumers tighten their belts and focus their spending only on the essentials classifying certain products and services as luxury.

But legal services are never classed as luxury. The deeper the economic crisis, the higher the demand for legal services. As individuals and businesses increasingly renege on their contractual agreements lawyers are constantly called in to assist with compliance.

Secondly, new regulations are never just introduced overnight, they are spoken about for months sometimes years to give the industry the chance to prepare for them. While some businesses within the industry foresee the regulations and prepare for them, others choose to ignore them and hope that they are not introduced. Those businesses that choose to ignore the regulations are the ones that are always impacted by the changes.

There are two serious problems currently facing the legal profession that has nothing to do with the economic crisis or the new regulations.

These are:

- Nostalgia
- The lack of business education

Firstly, the large majority of lawyers continue to strive under the protective kokum of a professional. This means that they are not subject to the demands for result that other business services are subjected to.

The dynamic of the legal profession has changed in the 21st century. The 21st century lawyer understands that there are two reasons why a client will seek his services:

- To provide answers to questions
- To provide results

The 21st century lawyer who makes 7 figures per annum:

- Produces results
- Provides answers
- Provides clear action steps for implementing his solutions
- Takes responsibility for the outcome of his advice

Secondly, most lawyers are of the opinion that business is common sense. All they need is to attend law school and when it comes to the business of law, they will wing it. Business is not common sense. Entrepreneurship is a skill like law. No one wakes up one morning and says from today onwards I am going to become a lawyer. To become a lawyer, one has to be trained. Like law, business is a skill and like any skill it must be learned.

Here is breaking news for you:

50% of all business start-ups fail in their first year while almost 90% fail in the first five years of establishment.

Have you ever considered why that is the case in this information overload century?

All the information budding entrepreneurs need to run a successful business are on the internet; so why do many businesses still fail?

I'll tell you why: many business ventures fail because they lack the fundamentals of a successful business...vision, people, systems, marketing systems and good business model.

> Many law firms are closing down and their owners seeking employment because they lack these five fundamentals of successful businesses.

What do all successful businesses have in common?

Whether it is HSBC bank in the city of London or a toilet cleaning business in a dusty New Delhi ghetto, they have:

Lack of any of the above will cause any business to fail. These five fundamentals can be found at the heart of every successful business. They are not just something that might be good for a business, they are the elements without which a business cannot survive. The aim of this chapter is to outline what a law firm needs to move from start-up to 7 Figure and why it needs those elements. Later on in the book, I will walk you through the process of developing these elements in your law firm to transform it into a 7 Figure Business.

Conventional wisdom has it that a business cannot make profit until its third year of operation. We have all bought into this lie. Let me assure you that, this is completely false. By applying the principle in this book, a law firm can realize profit from its first month of operation. The application of those five core elements is an insurance cover against failure.

Before plunging head-on into the five core elements, I will first like to answer the question: why does a business exist?

Why does a law firm exist? For the answer to this question let us start with an insight from David Packard the co-founder of HP computers.

He had no doubt that a company exists to make money. But while he felt making money is definitely an important result, he believed the real reasons for a company's existence must be; to accomplish something collectively; a desire to do something else - like make a product available or give a service and maximizing shareholder value. He said

> "the point is to win; and winning is judged in the eyes of the customer and by doing something you can be proud of. If we provide real satisfaction to real customers – we will be profitable".

> As Mr Packard rightly put it, a law firm like every other business exists to provide value to the customer. So let me ask; does your law firm exist to fulfil the purposes outlined above?

If it does not, then you need to begin to re-examine your reason for existence.

But how would you really know that your law firm currently exist to provide value to your customer? Here is your litmus test. The rest of this chapter is going to focus on the definition of value and the five core principles of a successful law firm, as I go through them, examine your own firm and see if your firm measures up to the litmus test.

What is 'Value'?

If the 18th century was about speed and the 19th century about quality, the 21st century is about two things:

What is value?

Let me answer this question with a brief story about my interaction with a consultant.

A few years ago I hired a consultant to provide some market intelligence for me. According to my briefing; I expected to receive a detailed report with the following information:

- SWOT analysis
- USP
- Competitive Analysis
- Competitive Intelligence

Instead what I got from the consultant was a document outlining how to carry out the exercises and information lifted from competing websites. After reading the report, I emailed him to complain that his report was disappointing. I told him I needed it revised. The fact is; if I simply needed information on how to conduct a SWOT analysis, all I needed to do was Google it. In this information overloaded age; why would I pay someone thousands of pounds to tell me how to conduct a SWOT analysis?

He contended that he had completed the work. He spent his time doing the work therefore I was legally obliged to make his final payment. He informed me that if I was not pleased with his work, I should make his payment then take him to court. Needless to say, I refused to make the payment and we ended up before the court. The judge ruled that the fact that he has spent his time doing the work I had to pay him.

I was shocked when I heard the ruling. I did not even bother to hire the services of a lawyer because as far as I was concerned the case was a cartoon. I reasoned no judge in his rightful mind would see that report and ask me to pay him.

But the judge in his rightful mind did rule that I had to pay the consultant.

Why did the judge rule against me despite reading the copy and paste report?

Answer: the judge like my consultant still defines value using the 19th century definition. Since the inception of professional services such as consulting firm, dentistry, accountancy, law etc. value has always been defined as the amount of time a professional spent on an assignment.

If a doctor treats a patient and the patient dies, the surviving relatives are expected to pay the doctor's bill before collecting the body even though the patient died. When a lawyer defends a client and the client ends up in prison, the client is still expected to pay the legal fees.

There is the old doctor's joke which I believe you all know that goes like this:

"The operation was a complete success. Unfortunately, the patient died".

Can you imagine taking your car to the garage and when you return to pick it up, the car cannot start yet the mechanic demand that he be paid because he had worked on the car even though it cannot start?

This is the dynamic of professional/client relationship – value defined in terms of what is good for the professional. However, as we move into the customer centric century, the balance of power is shifting; the definition of value has changed.

In the 21st century value is defined as a quantifiable benefit between the parties involved in a transaction. Note: it says a quantifiable benefit, which means value has to be sensory specific.

In the 1980s, quality was perceived as intangible and defied a precise definition. That was until Edward Deming developed a formula for measuring quality. Today like quality value is seen as intangible and so it defies precise definition. This is wrong. Why? Value without evidence procedure for measurement is not value.

I will pin down the definition of value further with views from renowned business experts. Starting with

"The Oracle of Omaha" Warren Buffett… *"Price is what you pay. Value is what you get."*

Value according to Ron Baker is the amount a customer is willing to pay for a product or service.

Alan Weiss – the consultant guru expands this theory. He says *"Our job is to improve the client's condition. We deserve to be paid for our contribution to such improvement." "Our fees"* he cautions *"must be consistent with the best interests of the client, not*

solely ourselves." He also talks about the client's condition which he advocates should be "improved objectively (e.g. profit, margin, market share) and subjectively (e.g. stress reduction, higher repute, seamless client interfaces); it is improved professionally (teams are more productive) and personally (they won't ask the buyer to constantly referee their conflicts). Thus, we have the two traditional measures of improvement:

1. Objective and subjective business improvement.
2. Buyer professional and personal improvement.
3. Speed of improvement.

Kazuo Inamori, founder of KYOCERA Corp. – *"Too many people think only of their own profit. But a business opportunity seldom knocks on the door of the self-centred. "No customer ever goes to a store merely to please the storekeeper."*

Samuel B. Pettengill – *"The successful producer of an article sells it for more than it costs him to make, and that's his profit. But the customer buys it only because it is worth more to him than he pays for it, and that's his profit. No one can look to make a profit producing anything unless the customer makes a profit using it".*

The above quotations by prominent business thinkers were introduced to emphasise the point that value is never in the eyes of the beholder, it is measurable and tangible.

Picture this scenario; you have a legal seminar in New York on Tuesday morning. You ring the airlines to book a flight for Monday morning and the airlines tell you that they cannot guarantee that the flight will be available and there is no guarantee either that you will arrive there on Tuesday; because as you know when an airplane is airborne about 90% of the time the plane is off course so they do not really know when it would arrive. You are advised to just show at any time at the airport on Monday morning and whenever the aircraft arrives you will hear an announcement.

You decide it seems you have no choice in this matter so you will just have to play along. On Monday morning you call for a taxi and the taxi company tells you that because it is Monday morning there is a lot of traffic on the road, they cannot tell you when precisely the taxi will arrive, you just need to wait; it will arrive when it arrives.

Furious with the "ignorant" taxi company you decide to take the bus. When you arrive at the bus stop, there is no schedule. A sign just reads: because of traffic on the road and there might be an accident and a lot of traffic lights on the way, it is impossible to predict when the bus will arrive. Therefore just wait at the bus stop the bus will arrive when it arrives.

> I can hear you screaming how stupid these transport people are, how can they say they have no idea when the airplane, taxi or bus will arrive?

Calm down; this is just a hypothetical scenario it would never happen. When you ring an airline to book a flight, they do tell you, your departure and arrival time despite the fact that when an airplane leaving from one destination to the next it is off course 90% of the times.

When you call a taxi company they do tell you the approximate arrival time of the taxi and when you arrive at a bus stop, there is a timetable.

Here is the interesting part of this scenario, a bus driver gets paid £10.00 per hour, and he knows the arrival time of his bus. The lawyer gets paid £200.00 per hour and you do not know how long it would take you to attend to a client.

Do you get the gist?

The reason why you are paid £200.00 per hour is because you are more highly qualified. You are paid for your expertise not for your time. If you were being paid for your time, you will just stay at home and get paid.

So how can you justify the fact that you cannot tell the outcome of a project yet a bus driver knows when his bus will arrive at the bus stop? The hypothetically scenario I presented at the top happens each and every day in law firms. Clients engage the services of a lawyer and at the end of the project neither the client nor the lawyer is capable of explaining the outcome of the project.

Do you still wonder why law firms are struggling?

To move a law firm from start-up to 7 Figure requires change in the lawyer's perception of value. That's because the definition of value has changed. Whatever service you provide, in order for it to be classed as valuable, it has to provide profit to your client and to your firm.

I am aware of the fact that in some situations, it is difficult to speak of profit or quantifiable benefit. However, just be aware that what constitutes quantifiable benefit in the eyes of your client is firstly that they are able to get their heads around the outcome of your solution.

My consultant may have used the court to define value for him. But remember the ultimate arbitrator of value in the 21st century is not a judge in the court of law but your client who is the recipient of your service.

What is 'Total Customer Experience'?

Marcus Buckingham in his book *"The One Thing You Need to know"* wrote that when he interviewed Sir Terry Leahy the man who propelled Tesco into a global brand, he asked him: how did he do it, how did he take Tesco from a UK retailer to the fourth biggest retailer in the world. Sir Terry told him that when he took over Tesco, the first thing he did was to ask and answer the question: who do we serve? This question is classic marketing 101: know thy customer.

When they established who they served, he put in place mechanisms for ensuring they serve their preferred customer. One of those mechanisms they put in place was to increase the numbers of check-out counters in Tesco stores. Asked why the focus on checkout counters, he intimated that part of good customer service was to show respect for your customer. He said there was barely a better way of showing respect for someone than showing respect for their time.

It is curious that Sir Terry chose time as a benchmark for customer service. This is curious because time is what is at the heart of law-yer/client relationship. Lawyers are paid per hour. Employees are paid by the hour and every single aspect of our lives revolves around the management of time.

What is interesting is that even though lawyers charge by the hour, their client's time has never been an issue to them. I re-member when I had just arrived in Holland from Africa…when I was given a medical appointment, if the ap-pointment was scheduled for 12:00, being an African knowing 12:00 meant 13:00 in African time, I would turn up at the surgery around 13:00. The receptionist would politely smile at me and say firmly Mr. Richards, you are late for your appointment. We will have to reschedule because your slot has been filled. I was always displeased with their attitude. I honestly thought they were being cruel. I could return home and die from my illness. The way they saw it if I was really ill I would have been on time for my appointment. After enduring this treatment a few times, when I had an appointment I made sure I was even fifteen minutes early.

But here is the interesting twist to the story, even if I was fifteen minutes early or dead on time, I had to wait at the surgery for at least half an hour. I felt because it was on a refugee camp that was why things happened in that manner. However, when I got into normal society I noticed that it was always the same when I visited my doctor or my dentist. When I moved to the UK I realised that it is the same. As a business person, on some occasions, I have to visit my lawyer or accountant. Most of the time when I visit a lawyer or accountant, I have to wait for at least fifteen minutes.

When I consult with law firms and ask them the reason they are unable to guarantee the outcome of their services, the response I receive from them is always the same: they do not know the circumstances of each client.

Many of those lawyers might have been practicing for five or ten years yet they claim they cannot predict the amount of time an appointment will take because all clients are different.

Imagine being at a hospital preparing for a surgery. A few minutes before the procedure the surgeon comes out to see you. You ask him how long the procedure would take and he tells you he could not say because every patient situation is different. Just imagine how reassuring his statement would be as you are being wheeled into the theatre to place your life into the hands of someone who is unsure of the outcome.

When clients engage your law firm, they automatically expect a certain level of professionalism from your firm. They expect a certain level of professionalism from your support staff. All of those combine to form the total customer experience with your firm. If those expectations are not met, you have failed in your duty of care to your client. It does not matter the level of expertise you demonstrate during the engagement, if the other aspects of your service do not meet your clients' expectations, you have failed.

In chapter three, I provide sets of questions you can ask your client before and after an engagement to be able to accurately determine the outcome of an engagement.

Dr Paddi Lund the Australian dentist who wrote the book "Critical Non-Essentials" said when he was upgrading his dental practice to a world class one; one of the guarantees he gave his patients was that if he was ever late to see them, he would give them their favourite drink. Dr Lund understood the importance of showing respect for his patients.

Part of the key indicator of excellent service in todays' legal professional environment, will then be the ability of law firms to demonstrate the benefit of their services to their clients. Success as a lawyer in this century of total customer experience will be measured by your ability to demonstrate the return on investment for your legal services.

Entrepreneur lawyers who want to move their law firms from start-up to 7 Figure will have to change from the concept of just providing client information they can find on Google, to knowledge provision. Lawyers who grasp this simple concept will easily move theirs firms from start-up to 7 Figure.

Below is a list of good customer service quotes that I hope will help you in your journey towards providing 'total customer experience'.

Walt Disney – *"Do what you do so well that they will want to see it again and bring their friends".*

Jeff Bezos, founder of Amazon – *"It's our job every day to make every important aspect of the customer experience a little bit better".*

Bill Gates, founder of Microsoft – *"Your most unhappy customers are your greatest source of learning."*

Sam Walton, founder of Wal-Mart, the world's largest retailer – *"There is only one boss. The customer. And he can fire everybody in the company from the chairman on down, simply by spending his money somewhere else".*

Mark Sanborn – *"Customers do you a favour by choosing to do business with you. You aren't doing them a favour by serving them."*

Jan Carlzon, former president of SAS Airlines – *"If you're not serving the Customer, you'd better be serving someone who is."*

Maya Angelou – *"People will forget what you said. People will forget what you did. But people will never forget how you made them feel."*

Bill Quiseng – *If your business cannot pledge "100% Satisfaction Guaranteed or your money back" something is broken. Fix it... No customer walks into your business, gives you money and then says, "Dissatisfy me, please...." Aim for 100% customer satisfac-*

tion...Delivering good customer service is business common sense. Your job is to make it common practice".

Value and total customer experience will be further dealt with in chapter three. There I will address the creation of new a market for your services. We will now dive into the four plus one business success fundamentals required for the success of your law firm. No law firm that implements these five fundamentals in their firm will ever fail. They are not just principles; they are the core principles responsible for the success of every successful business.

Visionary Leadership

What is visionary leadership?

Let's start with what visionary leadership is not. Visionary leadership is not passion or doing what you love to do. Passion and labour of love have become the coolest buzzwords in successful entrepreneur circles.

Most successful entrepreneurs advise budding entrepreneurs to do what they love doing or something they are passionate about. While these statements might make a good sound bite, I have never heard anyone give a precise definition of the word passion.

From what I know, if we all did what we love doing or what we are passionate about whatever the word passion means. I am not too convinced that we will have half of the people turning up for work tomorrow morning. For a start many people just do not want to do anything. So if those people were told to do what they love doing, they will just chill out in the sun and enjoy themselves. Secondly, most people are so stressed out with their jobs that given the choice they will leave within the blink of an eye. But they go to work each day because they have responsibilities, they have families and they have to survive.

So when I use the word vision in this context, I am not speaking of some outlandish utopian concept that will never be realised, I am talking about your mission and your reason why.

Vision means three things:

- How your business will look when it is complete
- The difference or contribution your business would make to the human race

- Your lifestyle at the end of the process

Let's quickly peep into the visions of some of the biggest visionaries of our time, who changed our world for the better.

Bill Gates on his innate vision for Microsoft – *"We had dreams about the impact it could have. We talked about a computer on every desk and in every home. It's been amazing to see so much of that dream become a reality and touch so many lives. I never imagined what an incredible and important company would spring from those original ideas."*

Joe Keenan, President of Atari & **Steve Jobs** – *"Get your feet off my desk, get out of here, you stink, and we're not going to buy your product". Joe Keenan, President of Atari, told Steve Jobs. That was before Steve Jobs told Pepsi executive John Sculley "Do you want to sell sugar water for the rest of your life, or do you want to come with me and change the world?"*

Henry Ford's vision to put America on wheels – *"I will build a car for the great multitude. It will be large enough for the family, but small enough for the individual to run and care for. It will be constructed of the best materials, by the best men to be hired, after the simplest designs that modern engineering can devise. But it will be low in price that no man making a good salary cannot afford to own one — and enjoy with his family the blessing of hours of pleasure in God's great open spaces"*

For most entrepreneurs the concept of a vision is the last thing they think about when setting up a business. Customer acquisition, cash flow and profit are in their minds in the start-up stage of their businesses. However, the opposite is true for successful entrepreneurs. For them the starting point is their vision because it is their vision that serves as the driving force. It is the unifying force or centre that holds the rest of the business together especially in difficult times.

Trust me on this one, business is difficult. After we have achieved our dream of building a great business that changes the lives of millions, we can rest with the knowledge that we have made a difference. But getting to that stage is not usually an easy task. This is the reason why you need something within you that will keep you going when everything tells you to give up.

Vision does two things; it pulls you through in difficult times and it forces you to think of ways of making your dream a reality. Many lawyers set up law firms because they felt they knew how to run a business. There were no compelling reasons why they had to open their firm. Theirs was not the desire to serve a specific course or help their community. In essence it was led by a desire to make a living. But the desire to make money is not a strong enough reason to keep going when the deck is stacked against you. When you have a compelling vision and a reason why, you will find a way to prevail no matter the difficulties.

Authors J. Collins and J. I. Porras in their bestselling book *"Built to last"* outline the essential roles vision played in the lives of successful companies that were built to last. Below is a quote from the book in relation to vision:

> **George Merck II,** 1950 – *"I want to ... express the principles which we in our company have endeavoured to live up to... Here is how it sums up; we try to remember that medicine is for the patient. We try never to forget that medicine is for the people. It is not for the profits. The profits follow, and if we have remembered that, they have never failed to appear. The better we have remembered that, the larger they have been."*

As you see the vision of George Merck II was more than just about making money or profit, for him it was about providing a service to his fellow human beings and making a difference.

Proverbs 29:18, the Holy Bible. – *"Where there is no vision, the people perish: but he that keepeth the law, happy is he...Where there is no vision, the people are unrestrained, but happy is he who keeps the law".*

Thomas Watson's vision for IBM – *"IBM is what it is today for three special reasons,"he starts. "The first reason is that, at the very beginning, I had a very clear picture of what the company would look like when it was finally done. You might say I had a model in my mind of what it would look like when the dream—my vision— was in place. The second reason was that once I had that picture, I then asked myself how a company which looked like that would have to act. I then created a picture of how IBM would act when it was finally done. The third reason IBM has been so successful was that once I had a picture of how IBM would look when the dream was in place and how such a company would have to act, I then realized that, unless we began to act that way from the very beginning, we would never get there. In other words, I realized that for IBM to become a great company it would have to act like a great company long before it ever became one. From the very outset, IBM was fashioned after the template of my vision. And each and every day we attempted to model the company after that template. At the end of each day, we asked ourselves how well we did, discovered the disparity between where we were and where we had committed ourselves to be, and, at the start of the following day, set out to make up for the difference. Every day at IBM was a day devoted to business development, not doing business. We didn't do business at IBM, we built one".*

Vision and purpose, beyond making money is the glue that holds successful businesses together. Without a vision the likelihood of building a successful business is almost zero.

How To Create A Vision For Your Law Firm:

There is no specific template for creating a vision, because there is no right or wrong vision. What is important is that a business has a reason for existence that is beyond just making money.

The following are questions that would aid you in crafting your vision:

- Why does your law firm exist?
- What difference is your firm making to your community or the world at large?
- What difference would you like your firm to make to your community or the world?
- What is the finished business going to look like ten or twenty years from the day you set it up?
- What is your end game for your firm:
  - Are you building your firm to sell and retire?
  - Do you want to build a firm that will last far beyond you?
  - What is your end game?
- What type of employees would you want to work in your firm?
- What would your family life be five or ten years from now?
- How would you want the firm to change your life, financially, emotionally, spiritually and physically?
- What is it that you personally want to benefit from the firm?
- How much money would you need to earn to live the life you want to live five or ten years from now?

Another aspect of vision which is not mentioned in vision creation is your customer.

There is the perception in the marketing world that the type of customer you will want in your business needs to be a part of your marketing process. While I do not disagree with this logic, I still believe that it is essential that we picture the type of customer we want for our business as a part of the envisioning process.

This is because as you develop the services you offer to your clients, you need to be able to clearly articulate the benefit of your service to them.

Charles Revson, the founder of Revlon once said that – *"In the factory Revlon manufactures cosmetics, but in the store Revlon sells hope."*

Chanel sells fantasy. In this commercial they provide images of fantasy with the caption:

"Share the Fantasy. Chanel...Buy Chanel and this fantasy can be yours".

What Are You Going To Sell Your Clients?

- Harrods Department Store in London sells class and elegance
- The Body Shop sells ethics
- Holland and Barrett sells long life

What are you going to sell to your clients?

What feelings are they going to walk away with when they leave your firm:

- Peace of mind?
- Long life?
- Energy?
- Smile?

The truth about buying is this, your clients do not engage your law firm purely for the return on investment, they also engage your firm for a feeling. What feeling are you going to leave them with? That should be a central part of your vision creation process.

How To Communicate Your Vision

The next part of the vision creation process is communicating the vision to the people around you. Your ability to communicate your vision to your family, friends and employees is the extent to which they will be willing to buy into it and lend their support.

Michael Gerber in his E-Myth series hammered this point time and time again, that all business is a family business. I did not understand this point until I had a business failure which resulted in the breakup of my family. It was then that I came to the realisation that every business is indeed a family business.

As entrepreneurs, when we make the decision to go into business, we are of the belief that we are the only people responsible for the outcome of the business. However, as it turns out in most instances, the people closest to us are also as affected by the outcome of the business.

One way or the other, our family is affected by the result of the business. If it succeeds, they reap the benefit. If it fails, they are likely to suffer the consequences. Our friends might not be as affected as our family; but they too are likely to be affected by changes in our schedule. And last but not least our employees. Their hopes and aspirations, their future and the future of their families rest on the outcome of the business.

Consequently, it is imperative that we communicate the vision of the business to them. To gain the support of those closest to us and encourage them to endure the long nights without us and in soliciting the support of our employees motivating them to give their utmost, we need to be able to sell the vision to them as we sell it to our clients.

Many law firms are in difficulty because of their inability to attract "A talent" lawyers. Many young and talented lawyers do not want to take chances on small law firms. They prefer to work with more established law firms where they are guaranteed a steady salary and benefits.

But the reality is this: many people that went into law did not do so purely for monetary purposes. They genially want to serve. The problem small law firms have is they lack the ability to sell their vision to those young lawyers. They have either not taken the time to formulate their visions or even if they had they struggle to effectively communicate it to others.

When I want to recruit staff, when they arrive for the final interview after they have gone through the preliminary recruitment process and I have made up my mind that I want to hire them, I sit them down and tell them my story. Where I came from, my struggle to come to Europe and why I do what I do. I believe deep down in my heart that if Africa is to be raised from poverty, it would require us Africans living in the diaspora with certain expertise returning to our various countries to help in the process.

I make it clear to them that my aim is to go back and build a personal development institute in all African countries. Therefore I must succeed and to do that we must provide the best service to our clients. For me it is a mission, that goes beyond just making money. And when people make the decision to work for me, they come in with the view that mine is not a business, it is a mission to save an entire continent. So we have to provide exceptional service to our clients, in order to win more business and get the resources to build schools.

Some of you reading this might think to yourself why should some-one who is just finding a job care about why I opened my business or my desire to serve Africa? Believe me, most people will choose service over money. I mean the majority of people in this world want to belong to something bigger than them. Your job as the visionary is to give them that thing that is bigger than them.

There is hardly a better way to communicate your vision to family, friends and employees. How you communicate your vision to those closest to you will determine their willingness to buy-in. Remember your ability to effectively communicate your vision to them would determine their willingness to buy into your vision.

To be able to take a law firm from start-up to 7 Figure, you need to have a vision of where you are going and effectively communicate that vision to those closest to you.

Why You Need Great People

In his best seller, *"Good to great"* author Jim Collins provides the business world with the most fascinating yet counterintuitive concept of business transformation ever in the history of business.

We have all been taught and made to believe that a successful business starts with a brilliant business plan. Jim Collins revealed in his book that for a business to have any chance of succeeding, it must first start with the right people.

Using the metaphor of a bus as the business and a company's CEO as the bus driver, Jim Collins recommended that prior to moving the bus from the bus station, the bus driver must first allow the existing passengers to disembark from the bus, only then should he allow the right passengers to take their allocated seat on-board the bus before attempting to move the bus.

What Jim Collins indicated with his metaphor is that it is only after you have the right people in your organisation that you should begin to plan where you are headed as a business.

> **The Jim Collins** concept – *"Most people assume that great bus drivers (read: business leaders) immediately start the journey by announcing to the passengers on the bus where they're going—by setting a new direction or by articulating a fresh corporate vision*
>
> *In fact, leaders of great companies choose to start not with "where" but with "whom. They begin by getting the wrong people off the bus and the right people on and into their right seats. And they stick with that discipline—first the people, then the direction—no matter how dire the circumstances. Take David Maxwell's bus ride. When he became CEO of Fannie Mae in 1981, the company was losing $1*

million every day. With $56 billion worth of mortgage loans under-water the board desperately wanted to know what Maxwell was go-going to do to rescue the company.

Maxwell responded to the "what" question the same way that all good-to-great leaders do: He told them, that's the wrong first question. To decide where to drive the bus before you have the right people aboard is absolutely the wrong approach.

Maxwell told his management team that there would only be seats on the bus for 'A'-level people who were willing to put in 'A' plus effort. He interviewed every member of the team. He told them all the same thing: It was going to be a tough ride, a very demanding trip. If they didn't want to go, fine; just say so but now's the time to get off the bus no questions asked; no recriminations. Out of the 26 executives interviewed 14 got off the bus. They were replaced by some of the best, smartest and hardest-working executives in the world of finance.

With the right people on the bus, in the right seats, Maxwell turns his full attention to the "what" question. He and his team took Fannie Mae from losing $1 million a day at the start of his tenure to earning $4 million a day at the end. Even after Maxwell left in 1991, his great team continued to drive the flywheel—turn upon turn—and Fannie Mae generated cumulative stock returns nearly eight times better than the general market from 1984 to 1999.

When it comes to getting started, good-to-great leaders understand three simple truths. First, if you begin with "whom," you can more easily adapt to a fast-changing world. If people get on your bus because of where they think it's going, you'll be in trouble when you get 10 miles down the road only to discover that you need to change direction because the world has changed. But if people board the bus principally because of all the other great people on the bus, you'll be much faster and smarter in responding to ever changing conditions. Second, if you have the right people on your bus, you don't need to worry about motivating them. The right people are self-motivated:

Nothing beats being part of a team that is expected to produce great results. If you have the wrong people on the bus, nothing else matters. You may be headed in the right direction, but you still won't achieve greatness. Great vision with mediocre people still produces mediocre results".

This concept runs counter to what we have been taught about business. In business school we are taught to create a business plan before the final decision to go ahead with a business is made. While it is logical to start with a plan before embarking on any endeavour, it is vital that we also remember that implementation of the plan will require the participation of people.

Let me just make a footnote here before proceeding, what Mr Collins means is strategy and tactic not the vision. The vision is the reason why you as the entrepreneur decided to start up a business. The strategy for achieving the vision is what will need to evolve and setting the right strategy requires first getting the right people on board.

In discussions with small or failing law firms when I asked why they can't employ good managers to manage their firms, the response I always received is; 'we cannot afford it.'. This is because most law firms view staff as an expense, which to an extent is true. The wrong staff are always a drain on business resources. However, the right staffs are an asset and investment. A single good employee can change the fortune of any business.

It is impossible to move your firm from a relatively under achieving facility to a '7 Figure' business without talented management, administrative and lawyers.

Therefore, if your goal is to move your law firm from whatever, your current revenue to a 7 Figure business, after your vision, the next step in the process will be to recruit the right management, administrative and legal staff.

As we proceed along it will become clear to you that business success is a formula.

To move your law firm from start-up to 7 Figure in twelve months requires the adaption of specific processes. In chapter four on recruiting 'A talent', I will walk you through the process of how to recruit only 'A talent' to you team.

Why You Need A Good System

One of the major reasons for the failure of a lot of law firms is the lack of a good system. In a mall to medium size law firm, the entrepreneur lawyer is the system. Everything is done according to his intuition and reasoning. However, as the business grows, his role needs to change. He too needs to grow along with the business. The failure of most entrepreneur lawyers to grow along with their businesses is one of the major reasons for the failure of their firms.

There are four stages of business growth:

- **Start-up**
- **Initial growth**
- **Momentum**
- **Breakthrough**

At each stage, the role of the entrepreneur lawyer is different. At the start-up stage he is the technician, the manager and the entrepreneur.

- The technician is the one that gets things done; the lawyer who actually carries out the client's request, market the law firm and even do the administrative duties.
- The manager plans and structures the work activities of the firm.
- The entrepreneur is the visionary, he dreams and is the energy behind the business.

In the start-up stage, the entrepreneur lawyer occupies many roles. In most cases he has a receptionist who doubles as an office manager. From the start-up stage, the firm moves to the growth stage. At this stage, the entrepreneur employs an office manager and maybe a marketing person to market his services.

With an effective marketing strategy, the firm now moves from initial growth to momentum. At this stage revenue is on the increase, there is a demand for more staff and better management. There is also a demand for a system because the technician (entrepreneur lawyer) gets busier, everyone and everything demands his attention.

By the breakthrough stage, the business is fully mature and everything goes according to plan. However, in order for the business to move from the initial growth to the momentum and breakthrough, it needs to have operational systems in place. Without robust operational systems it will be nigh impossible for a business to grow from stage two to stage four.

A system in a small to medium size law firm serves three purposes:

- It creates a framework through which every staff member will conduct their work
- It replicates the founder and gives him the freedom to work 'on' instead of 'in' the business
- It removes the chaos and uncertainty associated with most entrepreneur ventures

The Benefit Of A Robust System

Edward Deming – *"Confusion between common causes and special causes leads to frustration of everyone and leads to greater variability and to higher costs, exactly contrary to what is needed. I should estimate that in my experience most troubles and most possibilities for improvement add up to proportions something like this: 94% belong to the system (responsibility of management); 6% special....Good management and good supervision require knowledge of the calculations that will separate the two kinds of causes"*

He added: "If you can't describe what you are doing as a process, you do not know what you are doing"

Edward Deming was the person who transformed Japan from a war-ravaged country to the second biggest economy in the world.

"We believe that there was one major quality breakthrough in the 1980s,"

Quality guru H. James Harrington said. "It was not statistical process control, employee involvement, just-in-time, or total quality... It was the realisation by management that the business and manufacturing processes, not the people, is the key to error-free performance".

The key function of a system in a business is to reduce the dependency on people. When your work processes are recorded, anyone can be drafted in to replace a member of staff and they can conduct the duties just as good as the person they are replacing.

There are three types of systems in a law firm: Hard, Soft and Information Systems.

- Hard systems can be the equipment and furniture in the firm.
- Soft systems are Intellectual properties.
- The third, Information Systems supports interaction between all three systems and controls among other areas, financial information; marketing information staff productivity metric and so on.

McDonalds remains one of the most profitable businesses in the world today. McDonald's success does not stem from its hamburgers but its systems. McDonalds might not make the best hamburger in the world, but it has the best system in the world. When you go to a McDonalds to order a hamburger whether you are ordering it in the suburb of California or a dusty New Delhi ghetto, you will expect the same level of service. If you went to the countries with the worst record of customer service in the world, if you visited a McDonalds in that country, the service level would be completely different.

In order to create your own business system in your law firm, you need to answer the following questions:

- What outcome are we seeking to achieve?
- How can we measure our outcome?
- What would I need to know to achieve that outcome?
- What do I need to have to achieve that outcome?
- What results do my clients expect from me?
- What information do I need to fulfil our promise to our clients?
- What do my legal staff need to help them fulfil the firm's promise to our clients?
- What do my administrative staff need to do to fulfil our promise to our clients?
- What equipment will I need to fulfil my promise to my client?
- What additional resources would I need to fulfil my promise to my clients?

The answer to these questions will provide you with the type of information you need to create the requisite system for your business.

But without a good system that could automate procedures and create accountability; it would be all but impossible to move a law firm from start-up to 7 Figure.

Why You Need Good A Marketing System

Peter Drukker is a premier management guru of our time –
"If we want to know what a business is, we have to start with its purpose." Peter Drukker asserts."The purpose must lie outside the business itself. In fact, it must sit in society, since a business enterprise is an organ of society. There is only one valid explanation of business purpose: To create a customer. The customer is the foundation of a business and keeps it in existence. The customer alone gives it employment. And it is to supply the customer that society entrusts wealth-producing resources to the business enterprise. Because its purpose is to create a customer, any business enterprise has two – and only two – basic functions: marketing and innovation. These are the entrepreneurial functions. Marketing is the distinguishing, the unique function of the business".

Marketing is a vital arm of any business. Without targeted marketing no business would survive. The most important tool for moving a law firm from start-up to '7 Figures' is an effective marketing system.

The focus of every successful business has to be:

- Customer acquisition
- Exceptional customer service provision

In order to provide exceptional customer service, we first need to acquire customers. Marketing is the process through which we acquire those customers.

What is marketing? It is the process of making selling easy.

There might be some confusion as to how marketing makes selling easy. That is because in the minds of most people marketing is the same as selling. But marketing and selling are two distinct activities. Marketing is the activity that a business conducts that places it on the radar of a prospect and selling is the act of persuading the prospect to buy.

Marketing activities include:

- Advertising
- Website optimisation
- Brochure and leaflet

Selling includes:

- Sales letter
- Cold calling
- Face to face meeting (Point of sale)

In order for marketing to be effective, campaigns have to be well structured. The internet allows for the creation of cost effective marketing opportunities for law firms to market their services. But it also tempts them to engage in several marketing campaigns at once. Engaging in marketing on several fronts with no mechanism in place for measuring results often leads to a waste of resources.

A good marketing set up creates an opportunity for a pilot scheme prior to rolling out the process in full. In chapter two, I will walk you through a step by step process for marketing your law firm. Just be aware that a good marketing scheme is essential for the creation of a 7 Figure law firm.

Creating a 7 Figure law firm from start-up requires that you have the four plus one core components in place:

- Visionary leadership
- Great people
- Good system
- Good marketing system

These form the foundation upon which successful law firms are built.

Why You Need A Good Business Model

There is a fifth element which serves as the glue that holds the four together; this is a good business model.

Before Facebook, there were many social media sites. Why did Facebook manage to dominate all of them?

Before Google there were other search engines, today Google is 'the' search engine of choice, how did it happen?

Is Microsoft successful because they have the best operating system in the world? Windows is probably the least secure operating system in the world, yet Microsoft dominates its rivals.

Facebook and Google are successful because from the onset their founders made the critical decision of making their services free. They then found creative ways of making money from their services. Microsoft's success stems from their ability to form alliance with other big corporation and governments.

Businesses are not successful because of their industries; they are successful because of their business model. DMT Mobile Toilet is a privately owned public toilet company in Nigeria. The founder of the company became a millionaire by simply providing public toilets. This is a real life testament to the fact that the level of success that any business achieves depends solely on the type of business model the company adopts.

The importance of a business model will be further dealt with in chapter three.

A law firm will not survive without any of them. But the key word is survive, it cannot succeed. To succeed or to move from start-up to 7 Figure requires that a law firm has all five elements in place.

Chapter Two: How to Effectively Market Your Legal Firm

The author of "Rich Dad Poor Dad" Robert Kiyosaki once said a friend told him that most professionals are just a single skill away from being wealthy. That single skill is the ability to market.

He told the story of an encounter he had with a young Singaporean journalist who sought his advice after an interview. She asked him if there were a few tips he could give her to improve her writing career. She wrote well but she had not managed to sell any of her works.

This is the advice he gave…learn how to sell. She looked at him with a ghostly eye and asked: "you mean to say I should go and learn marketing"?

"Yes" he replied with a poker face.

"I have a Masters degree and you expect me to be a salesperson"?.

"Yes" he responded again.

Stunned; she looked at him with an eye of abject resentment. Sensing what she might be thinking, he pointed to her notes. On the title of the note, she had written Robert Kiyosaki: bestselling author. He said to her "you see what you have written there? It says bestselling author and does not say best writing author". Lost for words, she packed her notes into her briefcase and sped out of the hotel.

The journalist acted like a true professional. Most professionals view selling with scorn and salesmen with suspicion even those who have salespeople working for them, view selling as something that is beneath them.

Here is the irony and the reality. The most successful people in any field are the best salespeople. From religion, politics and medicine to accounting, law and consultancy, the most successful are those who are very good at selling.

As I completed my research for this book, I read some books written around the theme. I was convinced that they held answers to questions that I had to address in some chapters of the book. These are books that came highly recommended. Many of them are bestsellers. But as I read the books I could not help but think to myself that, there was really nothing in these books. The truth of the matter is; you could read a bestseller that has nothing of substance, then you could find some obscured books that you have never heard of and they turn out to be like a gold mine.

Why is it that many of the bestsellers are basically trash yet they sell so well, while really great books languish on the book shelf if they ever made it that far? Answer: the authors of the bestselling books know how to sell.

What is the bestselling book ever in the history of mankind? The Bible in nearly as many languages as there are tongues… And just in case you failed to notice, it is a religious book.

- Who are the best salespeople in any society aside from kids? Politicians.
- Who are the best lawyers? Those with the ability to use the media to put the fear of God in the judge and jury.

We all know of a lot of brilliant professors; who have developed great theories that have been responsible for many of our technological advancements; yet, those same professors struggle to pay their bills.

Look at Steve Jobs. He single-handedly transformed Apple from a small business to one of the most recognised brands in the world. You could ask 'how' or 'why'; the answer would be the same... because of his ability to sell.

How much is an iPhone sold for? £400! How do you think he is able to persuade people to part with their hard-earn £400 when they can buy a Samsung which is equally as sophisticated for less than £100? It must be his ability to sell.

The mother of all selling, which might probably go down in the Guinness Book of Records as the best case of marketing wizardry in the 21st century is the Beckham brand. At the pinnacle of his career, the likelihood that he could not be counted amongst the best two hundred footballers in the world did not deter the advance of his brand. Instead, his became one of the most valuable brands in sport; certainly the most valuable brand in the history of football.

How did his agent pull that off? It is the ability to sell. Like it or not, all of life is sales. We are constantly selling ourselves to the people we encounter. Kids try all the time to sell to their parents. You sell yourself each day to your spouse, employees and clients.

As an entrepreneur, you are first and foremost a marketer. Secondly in your field, you are a technician (lawyer). As long as you decide to open your own business, you are no longer just a lawyer; you are now a marketer.

There is absolutely no way you can move a legal firm from start-up to 7 Figure without knowing how to sell. That is the first skill you will need to learn. Entrepreneurship is all about selling. The success of your legal firm depends on your ability to sell. The number one reason most legal firms struggle is the inability of the entrepreneur lawyer to sell.

Are you by nature a shy person? Or do you look down on marketing and sales people? If yes; I suggest you consider selling your legal firm now and seek employment. Alternatively you have to study the things I am about to teach you in this chapter.

Remember I said study, I did not say read.

> In Value Migration, Adrian Slywotzky stated that *"A business (model) design is the totality of how a company selects its customers, defines and differentiates its offerings (or responses), defines the tasks it will perform itself and those it will outsource, configures its resources, goes to market, creates utility for customers and captures profits. It is the entire system for delivering utility to customers and earning a profit from that activity"*.

While the term business model is often used these days, it is seldom if at all, definitively defined. But a Chesbrough and Rosenbloom paper points out the following six specific functions of a business model

1. Articulate the value proposition – the value created to users by using the product.
2. Identify the market segment – to whom and for what purpose is the product useful; specify how revenue is generated by the firm.
3. Define the value chain – the sequence of activities and information required to allow a company to design, produce, market, deliver and support its product or service.
4. Estimate the cost structure and profit potential – using the value chain and value proposition identified.

5. Describe the position of the firm with the value network – link suppliers, customers and competitors.
6. Formulate the competitive strategy – how will you gain and hold your competitive advantage over competitors or potential new entrants.

Writing some years back, in the Harvard Business Review, Joan Magretta said that

> *a good business model answers more than Peter Drucker's age-old questions…Who is the customer? And what does the customer value? "It also answers" she said two fundamental questions every manager must ask; "how do we make money in this business? What is the underlying economic logic that explains how we can deliver value to customers at an appropriate cost"?*

I believe you can now see that the future of your legal firm depends on your ability to acquire and maintain clients. Also that sales and marketing are the lifeblood of your legal firm. And the extent, to which you are capable of marketing, is the extent to which you will be successful.

What I am going to give you in this chapter are the fundamentals of sales and marketing. You might be thinking to yourself as you read this; I do not need this, I can hire a marketing agency to do my marketing for me. Before closing this book or skipping this chapter, ask yourself the following questions:

*   What has been the return on investment of your marketing so far?
*   What is your cost per client acquisition?
*   How many calls did you get as a direct result of your latest ad?
*   How many of those calls had a positive result?

- What was the value in ratio to the amount spent for the marketing?
- What is your USP?
- Why do your clients come to you?
- When was the last time you asked them?
- What is your client referral rate?
- What is your client retention rate?
- What is the value of each client to you?

Do you see where I am going with this?

Let me give you two additional reasons why you should read this chapter:

Firstly, no one can sell your legal firm better than you. You can hire the best marketing agency from New York or London; they will never be able to sell your legal firm like you can. People buy from people. They might buy the brand, but what they are really buying is who is associated with that brand.

Richard Branson has the ability to hire the biggest marketing agencies in the world. So why would he chose to pull his own marketing stunts? Because he understands that people buy from people.

The reason why many ads use celebrities and 'A-list' stars is because people buy from people. The reason why KFC logo has Colonel Sanders and Uncle Ben's logo has the image of one of its rice growers is because people buy from people.

Therefore, what you need to be thinking now is how to enhance your image to the point that it is marketable and you are able to market your legal firm yourself.

Secondly the 95/5% rule is also applicable to marketing. 95% of marketing agencies are not that good. Only 5% can be considered good or excellent. The question now is, in the sea of unprofessionalism, how do you weed out the good from the bad? And here is another; how do you know what questions to ask and what result to expect if you do not understand marketing yourself?

Read on. In the end you will be able to weed out good marketing agencies from the bad and you will not have to waste your resources on marketing campaigns that do not work.

> *"Scientific Advertising"* one of the best marketing books was written in 1923 by Claude Hopkins. He made the case that advertising can be measured. In this day and age when we have at our disposal multiple tools for measuring the effectiveness of our advertising campaigns, marketing agencies still maintain that 50% of advertising is wasted. The problem is they do not know which 50%. Why do you think advertising agencies get away with that statement? They do so because most professionals know little or nothing about advertising.

It is essential that you understand marketing if you desire to move your legal firm from start-up to 7 Figure. The good thing is that you do not have to do the marketing yourself. But by knowing what needs to be done, you will know what questions to ask a marketing agency and most importantly you will know the kind of result to expect.

Plan Your Marketing Strategy

Planning is good for directing focus; market segmentation and measurement of results. However, your plan does not have to be a complicated or elaborate document that is difficult to follow and implement. It needs to focus on the goal, attack the target market and have a marketing strategy for achieving your goal.

There are three main points that needs to be covered in your marketing plan:

The Goal

The first step in the planning process is to set your goal. In this case your goal is to achieve a 7 Figure income in twelve months. So you place that at the top of the plan.

The second step is to ask and answer the following questions:

- How many clients would I need to be able to achieve a 7 Figure income in twelve months? You will be able to answer the first question by answering the second.
- What is the lifetime value of each client to us?
- Let's say for simplicity sake each client has a lifetime value of £10,000 per year to you.
- How many of those clients would you need per year to achieve your one million pounds?

You also need to remember that every client is not going to stay with you for the entire year. Therefore you need to make provisions for the fact that some might leave; hence your calculation needs to be based on the average lifetime value of each client.

The third step in the process is to segment your clients.

Market segmentation helps you to:

1. Know the lifetime value of the client
2. Know the cost per client acquisition

To be able to establish the lifetime value of your clients, you will first need to segment them into different categories:

- Who are those who are spending £10,000 per annum with us?
- What is their work?
- What is their age group?
- Where do they live?
- Which magazines or books do they read?
- Where do they shop?
- Where do they go for recreation?
- What groups do they belong to?

Based on this information you can now create your customer avatar. Note well that you can get hold of all of the above information in minutes. In this day and age, there is marketing software that can provide information on every household in any Western country. You are able to obtain precise information on how many people live in a household, what each person does, their age, likes and dislikes and a lot more.

By completing the segmentation of your current clients, you will have a picture of the type of person you would like to have as a client. Using that as a template, you can create your customer avatar.

What is an Avatar?

It is the personality that represents who your market or your client is. It could be the key to the success of your business. Put in another way; it is the process of visualizing your clients. There is nothing wrong with asking your current clients about themselves and what they think about you and your legal firm.

A client is a person. He might belong to a certain group, but he is still an individual with a separate identity. Therefore it is imperative that you create an image of the individual you want to do business with.

Here is what Peter Drukker has to say about customer avatar: *"There will always, one can assume, be need for some selling. But the aim of marketing is to make selling superfluous. The aim of marketing is to know and understand the customer so well that the product or service fits him and sells itself."*

Your customer avatar canvas must answer the following questions:

- What type of people are we looking for?
- Where are they located?

If your aim is to localise your services, the question you need to be answering is:

1. How many people in your locality are capable of parting with £10,000 per annum for the type of service you provide?
2. Which areas are they located?
3. Who is currently servicing them?
4. How are they being sold to at present?

What do the answers to these questions do for you? They clarify your goals and make it easy for you to focus your marketing strategy on your target market.

They also help you to know specifically how many clients you will need to recruit per month or per week to be able to achieve your goal. Whether you have an in-house sales team or if you decide to outsource your marketing, you will have a benchmark upon which to judge the performance of your sales team or marketing agency.

The last three questions brings us to the next part of the marketing process' competitive analysis.

How to Spy on Your Competitors – Competitive Analysis

Why do you need to conduct competitive intelligence before devising your marketing strategy? For an answer to this question, we will turn to Benjamin Gilad and Tamar Gilad.

> *"A formal BI [Business Intelligence] process is an organized, systematic, and on-going process and it produces high quality intelligence.... There is no other way to prepare against threats, or to identify opportunities early on, than to systematically, seriously, and competently monitor the environment...History teaches that behind every successful strategy there has been a tireless effort to collect intelligence...The intelligence collected in the first stage serves the second stage of the strategic planning process; the assessment of the situation by management... Assessment refers to the evaluation of key success factors. The assessment will point to the opportunities and problems in the environment. Those will generally be in the areas where the firm must do well to succeed. Each industry will have its set of key success factors"*

Sun Tzu put it simply but eloquently in the Art of War around 500CB – *"If you are ignorant of both your enemy and yourself, then you are a fool and certain to be defeated in every battle."*

"If you know yourself, but not your enemy, for every battle won, you will suffer a loss."

"If you know your enemy and yourself, you will win every battle".

I could not have said it any better. Competitive analysis is the key to gaining any form of advantage in a crowded market place.

How to conduct competitive analysis

The first step in the process of competitive analysis is the identification of your competition. You need to identify all legal firms in direct or indirect competition to your firm. They could be in or outside your local area. Remember the 'Butterfly effect'. These days a practice does not have to be in your locality or even country to compete with your legal firm.

To conduct your competitive analysis, take the following steps:

- Ask your current clients who else they currently visit for your type of service
- Conduct keyword search and find out which other practices are bidding on your keywords
- Conduct a Google search and see which businesses show up on the first few pages
- Use your Google Analytic report to see where your traffic comes from
- Use yell.com
- Use directories
- Use trade journals, look for the firms that are advertising your type of service

After the information gathering, the next step in the process is to analyse your competitors to know their strengths and weaknesses.

To achieve this you will need to find their:

- Marketing messages
- Offering
- Customer service provision
- Delivery mechanism

How do we get to know all of the above? Use the following tools:

First create a file on each of your main competitors. In that file you need the following information:

- Their website copies
- Their advertising material
- Their internet marketing campaigns on Google or MSM
- Their press releases
- Their services offering, past and present
- Their partners
- Their search engine and Alexa rankings
- Google alert

Also find their:

- Price point
- Accreditation
- Expertise
- Experience
- Profit margin
- Business model
- Business systems and processes
- Team competencies
- Support Material

You should also:

- Get on their mailing list
- Purchase their services
- Assess their delivery process
- Assess their customer service provision

After gathering the available information, you need to create two separate types of folders; one for the successful firms and one for struggling competitors. Based on that list you will know the course of action you need to take to make your legal firm successful.

When you make your offering ensure it matches or supersedes what the successful ones are doing. The reason they are successful is because they know how to serve clients. By understanding their value preposition and unique selling preposition, you will know what course of action to take in relation to your own sales offering.

By studying successful and struggling businesses, you will scrutinize their strengths and weaknesses. At the same time you will identify your own strengths and weaknesses. So you can craft your offering to maximize your strengths and make your weaknesses irrelevant.

The exercise gives a chance to have a good look at the opportunities in your market. There are always opportunities in every market. Everything requires some form of improvement and your job is to find what needs improving and make that a part of your marketing campaign.

Once you understand the strengths and weaknesses of your competitors, you can either decide to go head to head with them if you have the capacity or conduct disruptive innovation.

What is disruptive innovation?

"Disruptive innovation is a process by which a product or service takes root at the bottom of a market. From there it moves up market until it displaces more established competitors. The main features of disruptive business usually include lower gross margins, smaller target markets and simpler products and services that may not appear as attractive as existing solutions when compared against traditional performance metrics".

Process of disruptive innovation

- Introduces an entirely different value proposition to the marketplace
- Initially underperforming against established products and services in the marketplace
- Product or service continuously improves until it dislodges the existing players
- It is focused more on distinction in the marketing place in terms of superiority of service, valued, reliability, easier to use, and cost-effective.

Why use disruptive innovation?

For your small legal firm to have any chance of making a 7 Figure income annually you will have to quite literally woo clients from other legal firms. Enticing clients from already established legal firms is not an easy task; as businesses do all they can to protect their turf. Therefore disruptive innovation can be your best weapon.

Disruptive innovation needs not be a revolutionary idea or product. All that is required is just a little change from the way things were already being done. For example it could be an offer like an extended warranty.

When we started in the training business, it was already a crowded marketplace. Just by offering a guarantee that was focused on:

- The level of knowledge gained
- Behaviour change
- After training support
- Bottom line result

We were able to eclipse the market.

The three elements that must be present in order for disruptive innovation to be effective are:

- The identification of service opportunities that do not currently resolve the market pain
- The ability to satisfy clients' wants and needs better than the competition
- The ability to combine marketing, service and delivery

The one thing that you need to remember with regards to disruptive innovation is that every marketplace can do with some type of improvement. Your job will be to find what needs improving and offer it to the marketplace. In chapter three when we deal with the creation of your "Blue Ocean" – how to create new markets for your legal firm, I will detail ways of conducting disruptive innovation.

How to Effectively Position your Legal Firm Above Your Competition

As I write this chapter, there are now:

- 812,133,400 active Facebook users
- 100 million active Twitter users
- 150 million Linkedin members
- 100 million active Google plus users
- 294 billion emails are sent per day
- The average person is exposed to between 3,000 and 20,000 adverts per day.
- There were one trillion video playbacks on YouTube in 2011.

With so much information about, what hope do you have of your own advertising message reaching your target audience? In the marketing world, your message is not only up against your competition; you now also have to compete with close to 19,000 messages from other sources in addition to social media and email.

I personally receive about 150 mails per day. Of the 150, I manage to read about 30 that matters. The rest I just press delete. You can be rest assured that my own messages suffer similar fate when they pop-up in email boxes.

The question now is how can you ensure that your messages get past the filter and delete key.

Answer: positioning.

In their book entitled; "Positioning" Al Ries and Jack Trout described positioning as:

*"the first body of thought that comes to gripe with the difficult prob-
lem of getting heard in our over communicated society. And they
conclude that"the basic approach of positioning is not to create
something new and different, but to manipulate what's already up
there in the mind, to re-tie the connections that already exist... Positioning is an organized system for finding a window in the mind.
It is based on the concept that communication can only take place at
the right time and under the right circumstances".*

They provided a few principles for effective positioning:

- Ensure your message is targeted at a very narrow niche. Do
  not create a message that is intended for the consumption of
  everyone
- The message has to be clear and oversimplified
- The easiest way of getting into a person's mind is to be the
  first
- The most effective USP is the one already playing in the prospects mind
- Successful positioning requires consistency
- Never ignore the competition's position; when you understand the competition's position you can better position
  yourself
- The company stuck with the wrong positioning will never
  benefit from hard work, it needs to change its positioning
- Remember consumers are like chickens, they are more comfortable with the pecking order that everyone knows about
- It is an illusion to believe that the power of the product is derived from the power of the organization, the opposite is true.
  The power of the organization is derived from the power of
  the product and the position that the product owns in the
  prospect's mind
- Introduce your product before someone else has the chance to
  establish leadership
- If everyone else is going in one direction, try to follow the opposite direction

- Establishing a high-price position with a valid product story in a category where consumers are receptive to a high-priced brand is an effective positioning strategy
- Age, time and distribution channels are all positioning strategies
- You can reposition the competition by undercutting their existing concept, product, or service
- Ensure your name is generic and it stands for something
- Successful positioning requires a long term strategy
- Most positioning strategies are a search for the obvious. However, the obvious is easy to miss if your focus is on the product itself
- Adding information about the intricate and complicated details of a product or service is a great way of distinguishing it from the competition
- In positioning, start with what the prospect is already willing to give you
- Select a position that no one else has staked a claim on and use that as your position
- The focus has to be one of specialization to generalisation
- Remember to win the battle for the mind, you can never compete head-on against a company that has a strong, established position

To compete in an over-communicated world, if you do not have a multi-billion pound advertising budget, the most effective tool for competing is positioning. The above principles are meant to serve as a guide as you go about competing in your market. The internet and social media have now made it possible for even a small legal firm to effectively position itself against bigger legal firms. However, in order to succeed, the process has to be well thought through and the information above needs to serve as a guide.

How To Sell Your Image

Image selling is a very effective marketing strategy. When used properly it makes the selling process very easy. The essence of image selling is twofold:

- The image that the customer wants to portray by purchasing your service
- The image that the customer already knows that your legal firm represents

A person willing to spend a quarter of a million pounds to buy a Ferrari is not doing so simply because he wants to drive a fast car, he chooses to buy a Ferrari because of the prestige associated with owning a Ferrari. Every person deep down wants recognition and the appreciation from others. Shrewd marketers tap into the human desire for recognition and craft their marketing messages to fulfil that desire.

In his book entitled *"Breakthrough Advertising"* Eugene Schwartz describes this human behaviour as 'identification'. He defines identification as

"the desire of a person to act a certain role in his life and to define himself to the world around him—to express the qualities within him that he values, and the positions he has attained… All products may benefit from this power to define. But in particular, when you have a product that does the same job as its competitors, and is so priced that price is no longer a factor; then the prospect's choice will almost overwhelmingly depend on the difference in role that your product offers him".

I once watched an interview with a Ferrari executive. He said that when you drive a Ferrari, you drive a dream. This statement is so true. Most people who are into cars view Ferrari as the ultimate driving machine even though it is not the most expensive car in the world; but driving a Ferrari is like a dream come true for many people.

As you create your marketing message, your job will be to identify what roles and characteristics your prospects associate with your product and service. Whatever role and characteristic you chose must be one they already possess in their head. You cannot invent a role or characteristic from thin air.

Remember driving a Ferrari is driving a dream.

To be able to move a legal firm from start-up to 7 Figure, you need to be able to clearly articulate the benefit your client derives from using your services. In chapter three I will outline the process for doing this.

The second aspect of image selling is the association you would like your prospects to have with your brand. Image selling is the ability to market an idea that people cling to, an idea which in the end creates a positive perception in their mind about your legal firm. Certain brands are associated with ethics, healthy lifestyle, elegance, class, low quality, safety, innocence or quality. Those brands deliberately implant those images in the minds of consumers and consumers that those words resonate with immediately feel a connection to those brands.

- The Body Shop to most people represents ethics
- Harrods stands for class
- Victoria Secret is for love

When people enter a Body Shop store, they do so because it feels right. Products in the store were not tested on animals and certain individuals feel that by using products from there, they are swaying their conscience.

Many of the products found on Harrods shop floor can be found in many other stores in the UK. However, people shop at Harrods even though it is two or three times the price of other stores because it gives them the feeling of elegance.

When women want to go on a special date or when they want to surprise their significant other, they shop for their special bedroom lingerie at Victoria Secret. Wearing lingerie from Victoria Secret gives them confidence.

These retailers have carved a place for themselves in the hearts of shoppers. This makes them to associate their brand with the images cultivated by those brands. And that is more or less responsible for their success in the retail industry.

However, to effectively sell an image, the image you want to be associated with has to be planted in people's minds from the start. Some retail organisations flaunt their Green credentials. They sell carrier bags. Although they might be honestly doing it for the environment, because they had not done it from the start, people see it as an excuse to up their profit margin.

> The image that is projected could be that of the philosophy of the founder. Maybe your organisation could represent fun, love or a passion for life. It really does not matter. But it is important that your brand is associated with something. To maintain that image, your office and entire work environment should reflect that.

For example, say the image you want to project is that of a fun-loving organisation, your office needs to be painted with colours that are bright; cheery and it needs to be trendy and hip. If you want to project an image of an environmentally conscious organisation your office has to be designed and built to save energy. It should have Eco friendly heating, lighting, water and paper recycling facilities.

How to Implement Image Selling?

The following steps are effective for marketing your image:

Step one – Identify the image you want to be associated with. It can either be the philosophy of the founder or the organization as a whole. It first needs to be identified along with the story of why you want to be associated with that particular image.

Step two – Communicate that image to your office designers so that it can be incorporated into the office design blueprint.

Step three – Design your work environment to reflect that image - every fixture, lighting and décor in the office needs to be congruent with that image.

Step four – Ensure all your staff members are educated on your brand image. Their uniforms, actions and interactions with customers need to reflect your projected image.

> The main point to remember here is that as powerful as image selling is, it is a process. It is not an event. It is a process that needs to be consciously built into your marketing strategy and plan from the very start.

How to Create a Legal Firm Advertising Campaign that Gets your Phone Ringing Off the Hook

"Half the money I spend on advertising is wasted. The trouble is I don't know which half".

This famous quote attributed to John Wanamaker was made in the late 1800s and early 1900s. We are in the 21st century when the internet has made it possible to test our advertising before rolling it out. Yet many advertising agencies still cite this quotation as an excuse for not producing the desired result for their clients.

Claude Hopkins wrote in 1923 – *"The time has come when advertising has in some hands reached the status of a science. It is based on fixed principles and is reasonably exact. The cause and effect has been analysed until they are well understood. The correct method of procedure have been proved and established. We know what is most effective, and we act on basic laws. Advertising, once a gamble, has thus become, under able direction, one of the safest business ventures. Certainly no other enterprise with comparable possibilities need involve so little risk".*

As Mr. Hopkins has intimated, advertising is an art as well as a science. The ability to affectively merge intuition and evidence is what makes for a successful advertising campaign. To quote Mr. Hopkins again:"Advertising was a gamble, a speculation of the rashest sort. One man's guess on the proper course was as likely to be as good as another's. There were no safe pilots, because few sailed the same course twice. The condition has been corrected. Now the only uncertainties pertain to people and to products, not to methods. It is hard to measure human idiosyncrasies, the preferences and prejudices, the likes and dislikes that exist. We cannot say that an article will be popular, but we know how to sell it in the most effective way... In the old days, advertisers ventured on their own opinions. The few guessed right, the many wrong. Those were the times of advertising disaster. Even those who succeeded came close to the verge before the tide turned. They did not know their cost per customer or their sale per customer. The cost of selling might have taken a long time to come back. Often it never came back. Now we let the thousands decide what the millions will do. We make a small venture, and watch cost and result. When we learn what a thousand customers cost, we know almost exactly what a million will cost. When we learn what they buy, we know what a million will buy. We establish averages on a small scale, and those averages always hold. We know our cost, we know our sale, we know our profit and loss. We know how soon our cost comes back. Before we spread out, we prove our undertaking absolutely safe. So there are today no advertising disasters piloted by men who know".

This is the core of advertising; its fundamental function is to:

- take an unformulated desire, and translate it into one vivid scene of fulfilment after another.
- add the appeal of concrete satisfaction after satisfaction to the basic drive of that desire.
- make sure that your prospect realizes everything that he is getting—everything that he is now leaving behind him— everything that he may possibly be missing

My questions to you are:

- Which half of your advertising is wasted?

- What mechanism do you have in place for monitoring the result of your advertising?
- What was the return on investment on your last advertising campaign?

I really don't expect you to know the answers but the promise of this section is that at the end of it, you will be able to answer the above questions without blinking.

There is an advertising billboard all over Manchester. It is about Vodafone. Vodafone is one of the biggest mobile phone companies in the world. What do they have on the billboard? Images of Yoda from the movie Star Wars with captions such as: "We will turn your old phone into cash". Whenever, I drive pass those billboards I think to myself, who in this world would associate Yoda with making money?

The creative genius who designed the advert probably watched Star Wars the previous night. As he was watching it something clicked that the power of Yoda could conjure people into thinking that they could actually save money on their phone bills. Furthermore; his boss, probably a Star Wars buff too decided to approve of an ad that relates Yoda to making money and to add insult to injury, the purchasing manager at Vodafone who signed up on the ad might know absolutely nothing about the principles of advertising.

I had seen ads in the UK with images of Lionel Messi the world's most valuable footballer. Despite the fact that Mr. Messi is the world's best footballer, how many people in the UK really know his face? He could walk on the High Street on a busy Saturday, only a few people will recognise him. I have seen ads with images of Adriano, this was even after he had his troubles. How many consumers in the UK have ever heard of Adriano probably aside from his problems?

I brought these examples because they underpin the point that most advertising does not work because they are not properly done. There are fundamental principles which underpin good advertising. When they are followed, the odds are in your favour. However, failing those principles means that 50% of your advertising will be wasted the problem is you will not know which 50%.

This is what David Ogilvy has to add to this conversation:

> *"The use of characters known to people who see your television commercial boosts the recall of your print advertisements.*
>
> *Historical subjects bore the majority of readers.*
>
> *Do not assume the subject which interests you will necessarily interest consumers*
>
> *People see movie stars with who they can identify. The same factor is at work in advertising".*

To quote Eugene Schwartz again:

> *"Many campaigns have collapsed because they have asked their market to identify themselves with an unbelievable image…The men and women who comprise the market could not make the jump between themselves and the characters pictured in the ad. And they not only refused to believe the suggested identification but the disbe-*

lief spread to the performance claims themselves and killed the sales".

Vodafone, Nike or McDonalds can afford to live with a 50% ROI of their advertising. But a small legal firm like yours that does not have a fraction of their budget needs to ensure that whatever you spend on advertising produces the maximum return on investment. The only sure way of ensuring that you receive a return on investment on your advertising is to understand the fundamental principles of advertising.

The fundamental principles of advertising

1. The only purpose of advertising is to make sales. It is profita-ble or unprofitable according to its actual sales. It is not for general effect. It is not to keep your name before the people. It is not primarily to aid your other salesmen. Treat it as a salesman. Force it to justify itself. Compare it with other salesmen. Figure out its cost and result. Accept no excuses which good salesmen do not make. Then you will not go far wrong.
2. Human nature is perpetual. In most respects it is the same today as in the time of Caesar. So the principles of psychology are fixed and enduring. You will never need to unlearn what you learnt about them.
3. Use pictures only to attract those who may profit you. Use them only when they form a better selling argument than the same amount of space set in type.
4. Changing people's habits is very expensive. A project which involves that must be seriously considered. To sell shaving soap to the peasants of Russia one would first need to change their beard wearing habits. The cost would be excessive.
5. Prevention is not a popular subject, however much it should be. People will do much to cure trouble, but people in general will do little to prevent it.
6. We must learn what a user spends a year, else we shall not know if users are worth the cost of getting them.

7. We must learn the percentage of readers to whom our product appeals. We must often gather this data on classes. The percentage may differ on farms and in cities.

8. Competition must be considered. What are the forces against you? What have they in price or quality or claims that weigh against your appeal? What have you to do to win trade against them? What have you to do to hold trade from them when you get it? How strongly are your rivals entrenched?

9. Almost any question can be answered, cheaply, quickly and finally, by a test campaign. And that's the way to answer them — not by arguments around a table. Go to the court of last resort — the buyers of your product.

10. Consumers all over the world still buy products which promise them value for money, beauty, nutrition, real relief from suffering and social status.

Guidelines for hiring an advertising agency

Below is a list of guidelines for contacting an ad agency given by advertising great, David Ogilvy in his book: *"Ogilvy on Advertising"*.

- Don't delegate the selection to a group of pettifoggers. They usually get it wrong. Do it yourself.
- Start by leafing through some magazines. Tear out the advertisements you envy, and find out which agency did them.
- Watch television for three evenings, make a list of commercials you envy and find out which agency did them.
- Find out which ones are working for your competitors and thus unavailable to you.
- Meet the head of each agency and his creative director. But don't ask to see the work level of people who would be assigned to your account. You might find them congenial, but have no way of judging their talent.
- Ask to see the agency's six best print ads and six best television commercials. Pick the agency whose campaign interests you the most.
- Ask what the agency charges if it is 15% insist on paying 16%. The extra one per cent wouldn't hurt you, but it would double the agency's normal profit and you will get better service.
- Insist on a five year contract. This will delight the agency and protect you from being resigned if one of your competitors ever tries to seduce them with bigger budget.

How To Create Marketing Designs That Sells

"So with any other mail order ad which has long continued; every feature, every word and picture teaches advertising at its best. You may not like them. You may say they are unattractive, crowded, hard to read — anything you will. But the test of results has proved those ads, the best salesman, those lines have yet discovered. And they certainly pay"

The above summarises the concept of marketing design. When it comes to designing marketing pieces, there is the tendency to believe that beauty is great. The aim of a marketing design is not to impress people with looks but to enhance your marketing message. Most marketing designs don't work because those designing the piece do not understand the fundamentals of marketing design.

Most designers think that adding images in the design is to make it look fanciful. Fanciful designs are good for comics and children's' books. In the marketing world it is about the message. Every component that is included in the design has to serve the purpose of enhancing the core marketing message, not detract from it.

Remember Vodafone?

The one thing that needs to come to your mind when it comes to marketing design is simplicity. Some Apple products are not the best designed products in the world; however, they out sell all products in their niche. Why? Because Apple focuses on simplicity, elegance and functionality. Apple products are functional and elegant.

Google website is one of the top five high traffic websites in the world. Yet Google home page is simply its logo, and a few tabs at the top.

If you study the ads in top selling newspapers and magazines, you will notice that they are mostly in black and white. Also, most of them have no images; only essential information relating to the product or service.

When the London 2012 logo was unveiled; no one but the designers seemed to know what they had designed. Some people described it as a children's drawing, some said it was the symbol of an angry reaction. It was called all sorts of things other than a reference to the Olympics. The chairman of the London organising Olympic committee had to go on television to explain to the British public what the logo meant.

When a logo is designed for an event as popular as the Olympics and no one understands the design, there is a serious design fault. This is a lesson for you to pay attention. As you hire designers to create designs for your marketing, you need to ensure that those designs are clearly understood by your target market. The goal has to be that the design is:

- Simple
- Functional
- Clear

Why most advertising fail?

"Ads are planned and written with some utterly wrong conception. They are written to please the seller. The interest of the buyer is forgotten. One can never sell goods profitably, in person or in print, when that attitude exists"

The next time you create an ad that does not get your phone ringing off the hook, this should be your acid test:

- Was it created with the buyer in mind?
- Does the ad fit with your customer avatar?
- Did you take into account your competition?
- Is the design simple, functional and clear?

If you cannot answer YES to all the above questions, you already know why your ad flopped.

How to Effectively Use the Internet to Build Your Business in Twelve Months

Let me start with a disclaimer here. If you are looking for 'whiz bang' information on internet marketing that is going to revolutionise your business and make you a millionaire tomorrow morning; skip this section. I am not an internet marketing expert and I am not claiming to be one.

What I am about to give you is information I gleaned from my training with the best internet marketers in the world and strategies that I have applied to my own business that has worked for me.

I am going to provide you with two pieces of information: the myth and the key points to consider in internet marketing.

The Myth

Contrary to popular belief, no one makes money using social media. I guarantee you; the only people who make money using social media are those who teach social media marketing or those who create social media related products. There is no business or businessman who will testify that they used their social media account; made lots of friends and those contacts resulted in lots of customers for their products and services.

I am not saying that social media does not work. It does. However, the time and resource benefit ratio does not add up.

Social media and internet marketing is like the book or movie, "The Secret". No one ever succeeded with the techniques in "The Secret" yet it is so popular. "The Secret" taught us one good thing: the ability to use our minds to achieve whatever, we desire. But the part about just thinking and something vaporising is just not on. It has not happened before and it would never happen. You need to take action in order to get positive results.

It is a similar situation with social media. We just believe that by making lots of friends we will be able to maximise our chances of turning those friends into clients, customers or clients. It just does not happen that way.

Consider two important facts:

Firstly, anyone with a lot of time to spend on social media is not the type of client you want to have. They will not make you successful. The people who will make you successful and who are really good contacts on social media will not just deal with you without some form of introduction from someone they trust.

This leads us direct to the second point; people do business with other people. If you think that because of the internet and social media the traditional business model has become obsolete, think again. Blindly placing information on social media and hoping that it would result in some form of meaningful business relationship is the same as cold calling.

The difference is at least with cold calling you either have the chance to speak to the person one to one or to them on the phone. The problem with social media, you just carpet bomb and hope that someday, someone will pick up the phone and give you a call as a result of you cold calling them on the internet.

It is far more difficult to form the kind of relationship on the internet that leads to any meaningful business transaction, than it is to cold call in person or on the phone. One of the main reasons for that is when people see you or when they speak to you, they can immediately form an opinion of you – good or bad. It is difficult to do that on the internet. That's why it takes longer to develop a relationship on the internet than in real life.

The internet and social media are not great marketing tools however, they are marketing tools that can produce results when utilised effectively. So how can you derive the maximum benefit from social media? You do that by relationship building through contents distribution.

Key Pointers for Effective Use of the Internet and Social Media

The key thing to remember with internet marketing is this; content is king. The better the contents you have, the greater your chances of transforming your relationship into business transaction and cash in your bank.

There are two things to remember about social media and the internet. You can go there to make friends or to build your business. You can either use your social media platform to broadcast lots of junk about yourself that no one really cares about or you can use it to build meaningful relationships that would result in business.

What do I mean by that? What I mean is this; you can use your Tweet feed to send messages about what you ate and which part of planet earth you are or you can use it to provide valuable information to your community.

Most social media trainers and gurus advise that you place casual information about yourself on social media because people want to know you. No they don't! I promise you, the only people on planet earth who are interested in what you eat or wear or where you are could be your friends but more often than not they are people who have absolutely nothing to do with their time. And you don't really want to know those people because they can never in a million years become your client.

You want people who are so busy looking for money to pay for your service that they do not have the time to be nosing other people's business.

The reason I gave you the marketing fundamentals up front is this; marketing never changes. It does not matter what type of marketing vehicle you are using; by applying the fundamental principles up front, you increase your chances of success.

As I mentioned previously, I have trained with some of the best names in internet marketing in the world. What I noticed in all of them is that their success is not the result of their ability to use the internet better than other internet marketers. Their success is the result of their ability to merge internet marketing with the fundamentals of marketing.

> They devote a lot of time to planning. Firstly they clearly articulate their desired outcome. Then they complete a competitive analysis, test every aspect of their plan, position themselves well, then they use the internet as a vehicle for mass marketing.

The internet on its own is not and I repeat it is not an effective marketing strategy; it is just a vehicle that can be used after the application of all the other marketing fundamentals. You can never make money on the internet if you do not know how to position yourself well and design advertising that does not look like you are trying to hard sell.

Enough ranting let's return to how to effectively use the internet to market your services.

Now that we have established whom you do not want to target in your internet marketing strategy, here is how you go after the people you want to target.

Step one – Establish exactly the types of customers you want to target. This is marketing 101: know thy customer.

Step two – Establish what it is that they want. The people who can pay for your services are on the internet for a reason. They are not there for idle chat about what you ate; they are there for a reason so find out that reason.

Step three – Position yourself as an expert by providing them with information about what they want. It does not necessarily have to be your own content. For example, you could provide your community constant link to Youtube videos, articles or research report about information relating to their niches. And then once in a while, you can sneak in your marketing information. As long as they are used to receiving good information from you regularly when you sneak in your marketing information they will not mind.

The key here is consistency. You need to ensure you keep in contact with your community on a daily basis if possible, if not at least twice a week.

Ensure you stick to the major social media sites such as: Facebook, Twitter, Linkedin, Youtube and Google plus. You can register on as many social media sites as possible there are tools such as: Social Oomps, Ping.fm, MarketMesuit, Hootsuite and Tweekdeck that you can use for monitoring all of your social media accountants and broadcast simultaneously.

Remember four fundamentals with regards to internet and social media marketing:

1. No one makes money from social media except those who sell social media training and software.
2. To effectively use social media as a part of your marketing vehicle, you will need to apply other marketing fundamentals to the process.
3. Concentrate solely on the main social media sites such as Facebook, Twitter, Linkedin, Youtube and Google plus and you

can effectively use social media tools such as Social Oomps, Ping.fm, MarketMesuit, Hootsuite and Tweekdeck to monitor and broadcast.

4. Never, never post duplicate content on the various sites it would not help your website rankings.

Finally, use social media to draw traffic to your website. Valuable content on your social media account will draw more and more visitors who can then be converted into clients. Ensure that your website is well optimised for traffic. A cost effective way of doing this is blogging. If you blog once a week and link your blog post to your social media account then to your website, you can send unbelievable traffic to your website.

Effective marketing is all about the fundamentals. When you study the fundamentals and apply the use of modern tools such as the internet you can skyrocket your marketing results.

The key phrase to remember is: marketing fundamentals.

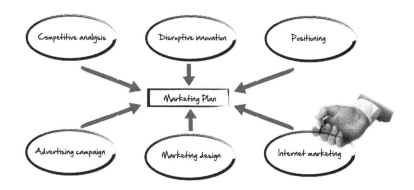

Chapter Three: How to Create A New Market for Your Law Firm

Why is "Blue Ocean" Critical for Your Law Firm?

As we go into what perhaps is the most important chapter of this book, I suggest you soak up the following quotations.

Ralph Waldo Emerson – *"Do not go where the path may lead; instead go where there is no path and leave a trail"*.

Charles A. O'Reilly III and **Michael L. Tushman** – *"The Roman god Janus had two sets of eyes—one pair focusing on what lay behind, the other on what lay ahead. General Managers and corporate executives should be able to relate. They, too, must constantly look backward, attending to the products and processes of the past, while also gazing forward, preparing for the innovations that will define the future"*

Karl Albrecht – *"The longer you've been in business, the greater the probability you do not really understand what's going on in the minds of your customers"*

Andy Grove – *"Disruptive threats came inherently not from new technology but from new business models."*

Buggy Whips – *"When an industry is at the apogee of its efficiency, it is often at risk of being made obsolete by new technologies or business models."*

Peter Drucker – *"No amount of efficiency gains would have saved the buggy whip manufacturers from the automobile"*

George Gilder – *"Knowledge is about the past; entrepreneurship is about the future. If creativity was not unexpected, governments could plan it and socialism would work. But creativity is intrinsically surprising and the source of all real profit and growth"*

No business can move from start-up to a 7 Figure in twelve months if it just copied the business model of its competitors. A business that desires to move from start-up to a 7 Figure operation in twelve months has to be inventive. It has to be different from its competitors and it has to lead the field in creativity.

As I developed the idea for this book, several questions bugged me.

There were:

- How is it going to be different, from other business books?
- What new insights could I bring to the discussion on business development?
- How can I really provide value and help you develop your law firm?

I got my answers to these questions when I discovered the 'Blue Ocean' concept...How to attract new clients. I was thrilled. Finally, I knew that I had a contribution to make. However, I quickly realised that just stumbling upon a new concept was not enough. I needed to translate it and make it relevant to the legal profession. As a part of this endeavour, I conducted extensive research into legal professions around the world to get a feel for business strategies that have been successfully implemented by lawyers that could be introduced to lawyers in the Western World. But, the more I searched, the more I came to the conclusion that the creation of a new market for law firms in the West did not really need some kind of ingenious idea. If a lawyer wanted to move his firm from start-up to a 7 Figure operation, all that is needed is a new approach to service delivery.

There are two areas of legal service delivery mechanism that I believe if changed would result in shiploads of new clients for the firm. The two main areas are:

Some law firms still define value using the 19th century definition. Then value was defined in terms of benefit to the service provider. The concept of value has changed. It is now defined in terms of the buyer. There is also some inconsistency in pricing. Here some providers still base charges on procedures rather than on the value of service.

It follows that if law firms changed the way they define value and their pricing plan, many law firms would significantly increase their business.

The rest of this chapter will show lawyers how to redefine value and structure their pricing to increase benefit for clients and grow profit for their firm.

Let me tell you a story!

Sometime ago, I took my son to Liverpool Children hospital for corrective laser surgery. As he was to be sedated we were cautioned that he should have nothing to eat for six hours prior to the procedure. We travelled from Manchester and arrived at the hospital around half an hour early.

After signing in at the reception, we were taken to the ward for preoperative tests. By around noon, the families were informed that the procedure would start in around an hour and half. At about that time, the consultant came into the ward. He outlined the plan for the day. He was followed by the anaesthetist who explained his role in the procedure. It was three o'clock and I had a question for him. I asked why we were given an 11.30 AM appointment for the procedure. "I have no idea" he replied and explained that his job was to anaesthetise but had nothing to do with arranging the appointments. "May be that's a matter for hospital management" he alluded.

Four hours had elapsed since our arrival when I observed that many of the clients who arrived after us had been seen and my son was listed last bar one client to be seen. I asked about time slots for patients. At the same time I pointed out that he was the first to arrive on the ward for an appointment at 11:30 am and also that he had not eaten for almost 24 hours.

"Who scheduled appointments? I asked the nurse. She said she had no idea. In fact she said her job was to carry out the nursing stuff and that was all she knew. She then explained that the procedure was not carried out on a first come first serve basis, it was the consultant who determined the order in which patients were seen.

Finally about five hours after we arrived, my son was called. Twenty minutes later he was back on the ward. Basically we had to wait for almost five hours for a procedure that took less than 20 minutes.(We had to wait almost five hours with a hungry child.)

What did I extrapolate from the entire experience?

Firstly, that there was complete disregard for the welfare of the children. Patients are told not to eat for six hours prior to the procedure. So children are expected to eat as normal the night before and involuntarily fast until early evening the following day. I think a hospital that is sensitive towards the welfare of children; would have scheduled the procedure for early in the morning if only to ensure children were not forced to fast for the entire day.

Secondly, since they already knew the amount of time the procedure takes and the number of children they had on that day, they could easily have staggered the appointments throughout the day to avoid the situation in which nine hungry children were locked up in a room for almost five hours. The entire place was a complete mayhem. Children were screaming, parents were losing their cool and medical staff walked around with no idea what to do.

Thirdly, it appears to me that those in the hospital management who made the schedule had no idea how long the procedure takes. This is because if they knew, they would have created a better schedule. As an adult, if you don't eat an entire day, what happens to you? You are right! Now you can imagine what happens when an eighteen months old child goes hungry for an entire day.

What do you think children think about the entire day:

The stock market? The economic crisis? Or maybe oil price?

No! They think about food. Deprive them of food for an entire day and you get the worst in them.

Why did I choose to start this chapter with this story? Not what you might be thinking. I do not intend to use my book to disparage the NHS. As an institution it is probably one of the best things that has ever happened to the human race. There is no other part of the world where someone gets sick, walks into the hospital and is treated; no question asked. I have been in the hospital myself as a client. The medical staff are great people, in a way I feel sympathetic towards them that they have to take the rap for bad management of a great institution.

Well, I started with this story for two reasons.

I merely wanted to direct attention to the core message of this chapter and the book in general. That is to say, professionals don't always live up to their profession. Some individuals in the NHS top management earn more than the prime minister. Of course they are so well paid because they are professionals, yet they seem incapable of organising simple appointment schedule.

Secondly, it is so easy to get the feeling that in the NHS an anomaly in professionalism is the norm. As mentioned in chapter one, the majority of professionals go about their business unaware that this is a customer-centric age. Put another way, they don't know that today's customer reigns supreme. Today business is more about total customer experience. The 21st century belongs to businesses that understand this simple concept.

When I interviewed lawyers for this book, I assured them that it is really easy to make 7 Figure per annum as a lawyer. Then proceeded to explain: all that is required to achieve a 7 Figure income as a lawyer is to make a move from a 19th century operation to a 21st century legal business model.

There are two pre-requisites for making 7 Figure as a lawyer:

1. Behave Like A True Professional

Here's how. Start working as a David Maister's true professional. In his book "True Professional" the author describes a true professional as one who cares deeply about his customers as fellow human beings. To achieve this and be successful in the 21st century, a lawyer must show that he genuinely cares about his clients and be willing to treat them as a human being.

During a discussion with a child shrink one day I asked her how she coped with the fact that she spent her entire day listening to children dumping their stress and frustrations on her. "It is easy," she said. "We have been trained to detach ourselves from the person". She said, it is like a medical doctor, when a patient dies he does not take home the stress that results from the loss.

I pressed further, but at what point do you realise that you are dealing with another human being"? She insisted that in her work she cannot take the situation of clients on-board. I still believe that when we deal with another human being, there comes a point when we shift from the protection of professionalism and really care about the person. If it's not for any other reasons than the fact that we all belong to the human race, this is true professionalism.

$$IQ + EQ + SQ = BS$$

My friend, like many professionals does not realise that a good IQ no longer denote success. Today, in most instances it is all about Emotional Intelligence (EI/EQ) and Social Intelligence (SI/SQ). In his book The Power of Emotional Intelligence Daniel Goleman says What most successful people have in common and most unsuccessful people lack is EQ not IQ. In other words with a good IQ you are expected to achieve a certain level of success. A high EQ changes that to extraordinary success.

All lawyers are presumed to be blessed with a good IQ. However, being intelligent is not enough to succeed in the business of law. To succeed in the legal business an entrepreneur lawyer also needs good EQ and SQ.

So if there is only one thing you take away from this book let it be this...your ability to connect with people, touch their heart and let your emotions show. The level of success you will achieve in your law firm depends on it.

> Malcolm Gladwell in his book "Blink" says that most people who claim medical mal-practice and institute legal proceedings against their doctors did not like them. According to Gladwell, doctors who did not spend a lot of time speaking with patients were more likely to be sued than those who spent just a few minutes extra speaking to their clients.

I agree one hundred per cent with the above statement because I had a personal experience of such a situation. The story I started in the chapter with about my son actually started in Manchester. He was born with his birthmark. Therefore the very day he was born, we had discussions with the hospital and were told that when he was six months old they will commence laser procedure to lessen his birthmark.

From the time he was six months old we had been in contact with the hospital about the procedure and all we got were referrals from one hospital to another. This went on until he was two years old. We received a letter from a hospital in Manchester for an appointment with a consultant.

We were hoping that they would finally tell us when the procedure would start. Upon arrival at the hospital, they carried out their routine medical checks and after an hour of waiting we were called in to see the consultant. When we entered the consultant's office, he did not even bother to greet us, He sat with his legs crossed as he spoke to us.

He informed us that the procedure could not be performed because the consultant who was to perform it had retired. He further explained that his successor had decided to return to medical school.

He admitted that he had no idea what was going to happen next and advised us to return home and wait.

The behaviour of this consultant infuriated us so much that after leaving his office we immediately lodged a complaint. His actions turned out to be a blessing in disguise because after the complaint, our case was dealt with swiftly and we were transferred to Liverpool.

I recall that during our discussion I remarked to him "you are too cold, you cannot treat people in that manner." "I am just telling you the truth", he said. He was probably right, but he failed to connect his heart to his words.

There are three sides to this story.

1. This is a procedure that we have been awaiting for two years, been posted from one hospital to the next and here was this guy sat with his legs crossed over telling us that he had no idea on the way forward, we should just return home and pray.
2. If that was all they wanted to tell us, why couldn't they have written us a letter or called us.
3. The manner in which the consultant broke the news to us. When we entered the room, he did not even make the attempt to acknowledge our presence. Then he broke the news without showing any kind of empathy or the slightest emotion. We met other consultants who told us basically the same news. The difference here is that they broke the news with feeling. They took time to examine our son, played with him and examined the spot before breaking the news to us.

You can never detach your heart from your work, as doing so will yield very little result and you will receive a whole lot of grief from your clients as the last consultant later discovered.

2. Change your Modus Operandi

Stop doing what most law firms currently do. What do I mean by stop doing what most law firms do? Well except you have just arrived, you will have noticed that a vast majority of businesses and individuals that use legal services are dissatisfied with the way they are treated by their law firms. Therefore, just doing things differently will differentiate your law firm from your competitors.

The aim of this chapter is to show you what you can do differently that would make your law firm standout and create more business than you have ever imagined. The core strategy of this chapter is not aimed at defeating the competition but making it irrelevant.

Wouldn't you love to be in a situation in which competition does not matter? Well I am about to show you how to create a position that ensures that from this day forward, your competition is as good as non-existent. There is a way to put your law firm out of reach of all competition which is through the creation of a "Blue Ocean" strategy.

What is a "Blue Ocean"?

The name "Blue Ocean" was coined by W. Chan Kim and Renée Mauborgne in their bestselling book entitled "Blue Ocean Strategy". In their book, they declare that "Blue Ocean" is about untapped market space, demand creation, and the opportunity for highly profitable growth".

They introduced the concept of a "Red Ocean". Red Oceans are all of the industries currently in existence. They are the current market-place where industry boundaries are defined and accepted, and the competitive rules of the game are well known. In the Red Ocean, companies fight to outperform each other for a greater share of the market. As the competition increases, products turn to commodities, profits are eroded and the prospect for growth diminishes.

So in order to create new opportunities for growth, organisations are encouraged to implement the "Blue Ocean" strategy. This would lead them to focus more on developing new markets for their products and services.

As a law firm, if your focus is on beating your competition, you are literally fighting a losing battle. With the advancement in technology and service provision software, productivity has increased tenfold resulting in supply outpacing demand with both products and services. Meanwhile, the demand curve has remained static as the internet make it possible for the factors of distribution once held by a few to now be open to anyone with an internet connection.

These days, an individual can operate a multi-million pound law firm from the back of his car as long as he has an internet connection. As these changes take place marketing experts and most professionals keep devising ways of outsmarting the competition instead of developing innovative ways of neutralising them.

Despite this increase in availability of products and services, the market for legal services remains untapped as most lawyers maintain the old ways of doing business as highlighted in my story above.

The concept of value and value pricing remains something of an enigma in the legal profession. The habit of hourly rates which removes all risk from the law firm to the client remains the norm despite the fact that customers has continue to voice their displeasure at this practice.

Hourly rates do not only disadvantage the client, it also robs law firms of their ability to make maximum profit and limit their creativity and ingenuity. In order for law firms to move from start-up to 7 Figure, they will need to desist from the old way of doing business to a 21st century business model that focuses on total customer experience. The old legal business model is unsuitable for a 21 century customer centric business environment that emphasis total customer experience above all things.

Law firms that want to move from start up to 7 Figure have to introduce a "Blue Ocean" strategy that will not only make their competition irrelevant but will also create a whole new market for their services.

How to Create a "Blue Ocean" Strategic Canvas for a Law firm

In their book "Blue Ocean", Chan and Renée provided a framework for the creation of a "Blue Ocean" strategy for commerce and industry. In the rest of this chapter, I will endeavour to show you how to apply these lessons to create your own "Blue Ocean" strategy canvas for your law firm.

Step one – Answer the following questions:

- What factors does the legal profession take for granted, that should be eliminated?
- Which aspects should be reduced well below the legal profession's standard?
- Which factors should be raised well above the legal profession's standard?
- Which factors should be created that the legal profession has never offered?
- What are the alternative industries to the legal profession?
- Why do customers trade across the legal profession?
- What are the strategic groups in the legal profession?
- Why do clients trade up for the higher group, and why do they trade down for the lower one?
- Is there a chain of buyers in the legal profession?
- On which buyer group does the legal profession typically focus?
- If you shifted the buyer group of the legal profession, how could you unlock new value?
- What is the context in which legal service is used?
- What happens before, during, and after you provide legal services?
- Can you identify what issues keep your clients awake at night?

- How can you eliminate those problems through a complementary product or service offering?
- Does the legal profession compete on functionality or emotional appeal?
- What are the take up hurdles in rolling out a "Blue Ocean" strategy?
- By what percentage point would your "Blue Ocean" strategy increase productivity for your target market?
- If you compete on emotional appeal, what elements can you take out to make it functional?
- If you compete on functionality, what elements can be added to make it emotional?

Step two – Focus, divergence, and a compelling tagline

Once you decide the "Blue Ocean" strategic canvas that is right for your law firm, marketing must come to the fore. For yours might be the best service in the world but if you are unable to communicate its true value, you will not be well placed to attract new clients.

It is therefore central to the design of a new service that a lot of attention is given to Focus, Divergence and Tagline. When a company's value curve lacks focus, its cost structure tends to be high and its business model complex. When it lacks divergence, it gets locked into a me-too strategy with no reason to stand apart in the marketplace. Where it lacks compelling tagline that speak to buyers, it is likely that it is internally driven or simply an example of innovation gone wrong. Commercial potential is low and it has no natural take-off capability.

Do not underestimate the difficulties of marketing a new service. To change people's perception from what they are already used to can be extremely difficult. That's why it is advisable that the marketing aspect of the service is considered as the service is being designed.

Step three – Focus on:

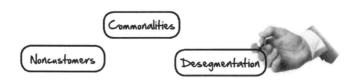

Chan and Renée also wrote in the "Blue Ocean" that there are three tiers of noncustomers that can be converted to customers:

- The first tier is buyers who purchase your offering out of necessity.
- The second tier is buyers who refuse to use your industry offering.
- The third are those who have never thought of your industry offering as an option to them.

By creating a service offering that will appeal to any of the above noncustomer groups, a law firm can create a brand new market for its services.

Step four – Segment your market:

There is a tendency for most small law firms to attempt to appeal to all people. They believe that by appealing to a broad spectrum of people it would increase their client base. While this may be true, there is the propensity to engage in a bloody "Red Ocean" strategy with the competition.

In the "Blue Ocean" strategy, specialisation is the key. With this approach you aim at a section of the market that no other law firm has hold on. In chapter two on marketing we mentioned customer avatar. By creating a customer avatar and concentrating your marketing effort on your target market, you stand the chance of dominating the niche you created.

Imagine if you advertise that you ran a legal service for only security firms, where do you think all the security firms will go for their legal needs? Yes you are right to you, to your law firm. There are some very obscure business sectors that many other lawyers might have never thought of, but those sectors might be a multi-billion pound a year industry. If you can identify such businesses and concentrate only on them, you will create "Blue Ocean" from completely nothing.

Here is the most important thing about specialisation. By focusing on a specific industry, you have the opportunity to learn more about the industry than people who are in the industry. When you focus and study an industry, you might seldom meet a prospect who is more knowledgeable about the industry than you are. And when you go to sell to someone from that industry, you will be able to speak the language they understand and understand their own industry lingo. Just think about how it makes people feel when you speak to them in their native language, that is how a prospect feels when he meets a lawyer who speaks to him in his industry lingo. But you can only do that when you specialise.

I am going to let you into a secret now. This is a gem if you got only this information from this book, it would be worth the money you spent to buy it and the time you took to read it.

Ready? Here it comes: if you can describe a prospect's problem better than they can describe it, you will never lose a sale. This information is so critical to success in the legal business that it is worth repeating: if you can describe a prospect problem better than they can describe it, you will never lose a sale.

How would you be able to describe a prospect's problem better than him? By specialising and studying every information relating to your niche. When you go to a doctor and you are explaining to him your symptoms and the doctor starts to ask you questions that indicate to you that he gets what you are talking about, how do you feel when the doctor prescribes a medication for you? Well, that is how a prospect feels when you can describe his problems better than him.

I will now address two specific areas in your legal services which I am confident if you concentrate on you can easily create a "Blue Ocean" in your industry. I am concentrating on these two areas because these are the areas that most professional service providers neglect the most and just by getting these two areas right, you can easily create a law firm "Blue Ocean".

The areas are:

Legal value provision

Legal strategic pricing

The Value Innovation Strategy Canvas

How to use value to create new markets for your law firm

The story I told at the beginning about my son's situation, might look like an anomaly but it is not. This is the type of experience most people encounter when dealing with professionals, medical or otherwise. One may say it is the NHS, it is the public sector so what do you expect? But the issue here is – it is not because it is the public sector. Sadly, the cause is because it is a professional service.

The fact is, I could have told the story of an accountant whom I paid to prepare a financial forecast. After he had completed it, I discovered there were some figures that were wrong. I asked him to rectify them; he insisted that he be paid for the corrections as it would require a few more hours of his time. I am not kidding.

All of the formula were already in his system all he needed to do was change some figures which would have taken him less than a quarter of an hour. As a professional, he did not see things that way. He preferred losing a client.

I went to another accountant, his fees for the entire job were less than my former accountant. Around the same time I had listened to an audio book entitled 'Anyone can do it' written by Duncan Bannatyne one of UK's most celebrated self-made multi-millionaire.

In his book, he speaks about his nightmarish encounter with professionals from the City of London when he was about to float his company. He tells the story of a particular incident in which he received an invoice from one of his brokers for travelling expenses.

When he received the bill he could not believe what he was seeing. He had travelled with the broker, paid for the cost of travelling including their meals on the train.

So then why charge for travel expenses? He called the brokerage firm seeking answers to the reason why he was being charged travel expenses when he footed all the bills throughout the journey. The response was a clear...that is the way things have always been done... So Bannatyne's advice for people listening to the audio book is... if they ever have to deal with professionals: lawyers, accountants, lawyers etc. be sure to agree the outcome and cost at the very beginning.

Armed with this information, when I met the second accountant, I made sure we agreed fees and outcome up front. As a result of this agreement, he completed the work to my satisfaction and on budget.

But here is the twist!

The following year, I asked this same accountant to complete the same task for us. Because he had done it for us the previous year, I did not bother to discuss fees with him. In my mind it was either going to be the same amount or at most one or two hundred pounds above the previous year's fees.

Guess what! I was dead wrong.

I received a bill that was more than ten times the previous amount for the same work that he had done a year early. When I received the invoice I was shocked. Only because I made the fatal mistake of not negotiating the fees with him up front, he had taken advantage of my trust in him.

To drive home this point, let me relay another story.

We completed a job for a client and we were not paid. We both had the same factoring company therefore, I knew it was not a matter of them not having the funds to pay us, they just wanted to delay payment. I went to a legal firm that I knew. We provided security for an office building that housed different businesses. One of them was a legal firm. Dealing with these guys almost on a daily basis, I felt more comfortable with them. I knew they were not going to be particularly cheap. However, I felt since they knew me personally, they would handle my case effectively.

Here again I was dead wrong!

I went directly to one of the partners who directed me to one of his junior lawyer. Like most professionals he told me he did not know how much the entire case was going to cost me, but that I needed to provide him with a deposit of £500. Knowing how much was at stake, I promptly gave him a cheque for the said amount. The following day I provided him all the documentation he requested and he promised to get in touch with the company that very day.

Two weeks later, I had not heard anything from the lawyer. I tried contacting him to no avail. At about the third week, I walked into his office to ask for a progress report. He informed me that he had not heard from the debtor company yet. However, from the way he spoke to me, I sensed he was being dishonest. So I decided to contact another firm of solicitors. I remembered that sometime ago I had paid them only £10.00 for helping me with a similar matter. This time within forty-eight hours the debtor company sent us a cheque for the full amount. I confirmed that my instinct was right. The first company had done nothing. Needless to say I contacted the partner I spoke with to request the return of my deposit and threatened to get the Legal Ombudsman involved if my deposit was not returned.

The above examples are not of public sector organisations. They refer to private professional companies that fail to live up to their promises. And as I mentioned previously, these cases are not the exception; they are the norm. Most professional organisations have not woken up to the fact that we live in a century in which the definition of value has changed.

The kind of relations between professionals and clients that passed as good in the 19th century are just not good enough for 21st century. Firstly, the emphasis of the consumer has changed. It is no longer about speed and quality. It is now all about total customer experience. The experience clients have when they interact with your law firm is what this century is all about.

Consumers are smarter now. Most people have so much information at their disposal it is unbelievable. My son is three years old and except for his corrective laser surgery, we have never taken him to the hospital or GP surgery. Whenever, there is an issue with him, my ex just Google his symptoms and she receives lots of information about what it might be and how it can be treated. She goes to the pharmacy buys the necessary medications give it to him and he gets better.

She is not alone in doing this, many professional people now just Google their symptoms or go onto forums when they are not feeling well and someone tells them what to do. Even if they go to the doctor, most of the time they already have an idea of what it might be. All they need is a confirmation from the doctor.

I see the same in retail. There is news of the UK High Street disappearing as thousands of retail businesses bust. The most common blame has been the economy or the housing bobble bust. But the reality is the current retail crisis has little to do with the economy or housing crisis. It has everything to do with an industry that has not yet realised that the definition of value in the 21st century has changed.

The only concept of value that is common in the retail industry is price reduction. Most retailers believe that to entice customers to their stores they must discount prices or make special sales offers. But a vast majority of shoppers do not buy on the basis of price. Most people go to a store to get a feel of the merchandise and the total customer experience. Most of them are professionals and those with the means to buy big ticket items would have already researched and decided on the purchase over the internet. They know everything that is to be known about the merchandise. Like patients visiting their doctors, they only want someone to confirm what they already know. But because the retail industry is focused on price, they fail to grasp this simple concept. This is one reason why they are losing sales to the internet. If the staff in the stores are unable to answer customer questions, customers might as well take their chances on the internet.

The entertainment retailer Richer Sound makes the highest profit, per square foot, in the world. In fact, the Gunnies Book of Records lists the company as the most profitable retailer, per square foot in the world. As it happens, they continue to top the 'Which Survey', as the company with the most knowledgeable retail staff in industry. Do you see the link between their knowledgeable staff and their profit margin? In the final analysis, when all is said and done, people want to do business with other people, not on the internet, but they want to do business with people capable of answering their questions.

Why have I given the above examples? Just to make this simple point. To create a "Blue Ocean" strategy or to put it another way, creating a new market for your law firm is very easy these days. All that is required is the redefinition of your value proposition to take into account your clients' perception of value. Not your perception which has been the case in the last few centuries, but that of your clients.

What is your clients' perception of value, today? For the answer to this question, I turned to Alan O. Ebenstein and Carl Menger:

> *"Value is nothing inherent in goods, no property of them. Value is a judgment economizing men make about the importance of the goods at their disposal for the maintenance of their lives and well-being. Hence value does not exist outside the consciousness of men...The value of goods ... is entirely subjective in nature"*

The value of goods Ebenstein and Menger says arises from *"the relationship of goods to our needs, and is not inherent in the goods themselves..."Objectification of the value of goods is entirely subjective in nature and that has contributed very greatly to confusion about the basic principles of our science..."The importance that goods have for us and which we call value is merely imputed (Menger 1976: 120–121:139)".*

Adam Smith expanded on this concept further by saying:

> *"both the buyer and the seller must gain from an exchange, or it will not take place. Were this not so, a contractor could build any type of house he wanted, hire incompetent and lazy workers, tally up his costs, add a desired profit, and still receive his full price".*

In the 'The Wealth of Nations' Mr. Smith adds

> *"Nothing is more useful than water: but it will purchase scarce anything... A diamond, on the contrary, has scarce any value in use; but a very great quantity of other goods may frequently be had in exchange for it"*

In his book Implementing Value Pricing, Ron Baker defines value as:

"what customers think they are buying, what they consider value is decisive—it determines what a business is, what it produces, and whether it will prosper. And what customers buy and consider value is never a product. It is always utility, that is, what a product or service does for them".

Baker further explains that there are tangible and intangible values.

Tangible values include the following:

- The size of the tax dispute, court case, risk exposure, size of the deal, economic impact on sales, profits.
- Increasing the customer's revenue, growth rate, profit, return on investment (ROI), market share
- Customer or team member loyalty, efficiency, effectiveness, cash flow
- Reducing the customer's expense, risk, turnover, bureaucracy
- Improving customer's process, systems, technology, information, and technical quality.

The following are example of intangible values:

- Specialist expertise or knowledge Unique social capital of the firm
- Brand and/or reputation of the firm
- Specialized proprietary technology (not possessed by competitors.)
- Opportunity to achieve a unique result given time circumstances and specialized knowledge
- Reducing risk to the customer through business model innovations—offering fixed prices, payment terms, service and price guarantees, risk-sharing pricing strategies
- Minimizing risk to the customer on the engagement itself
- Providing education to the customer
- Assisting the customer in mitigating future risk
- Knowledge elicitation—transferring specialized knowledge to the customer so they can develop their own.

- Decrease conflict, complaints, time or effort, increase morale, image, customer service and reputation
- Nurture the relationship with the firm, including comfort, convenience, and peace of mind
- Developing customer strategy, business model innovation, product or service design, Total Quality Service.

A business book will not be complete without a quote from Peter Drucker. The management guru writes *"What customers think they are buying and what they consider value is decisive… it determines what a business is, what it produces, and whether it will prosper."* He also holds the view that *what customers buy and consider value, is never a product. Instead, it is always what a product or service does for them. I cannot dispute his notion that the result of a school is an educated student so too is a cured client to a hospital or a 'saved soul' to a church. I wonder who can. Further Drucker maintains that "business exists to create wealth for its customers."*

What the above management and marketing guru confirms is that value is not what most lawyers now perceive it to be. Real value has to be for the benefit of both buyer and seller. However, if the service provided does not have any quantifiable benefit for the buyer; then it is of no value to the customer.

Moment of Truth (MOT)

There is yet another customer valuation concept. It is known as Moment of Truth (MOT). It was introduced by Karl Albrecht, one of the founders of the Total Quality Service (TQS) movement in the United States. Mr Albrecht defined MOT as 'any episode in which the customer comes into contact with the organization and gets an impression of its service.

Each MOT is a minor event. But as Baker explains over time each interaction is like a pebble placed on a scale, with one side representing service excellence and the other mediocre service. Sooner or later, the scale tips in one direction. According to Baker each MOT is linked to a distinctive result. He lists them as Neutral (rarest); Positive (moments of magic) and Negative (moments of misery) experiences. Few customers if any hold a neutral perception of an organisation but Baker advises that:

> "No MOT should ever be taken for granted, for no matter how small it may be, in the long run, each one determines the destiny of your firm...Even mundane thing as how accessible is your parking affects a customer's overall experience of dealing with your firm".

- The question you need to be asking yourself as you read the above is: what is the Moment of Truth for your law firm?
- What experience does your client leave with after interacting with your law firm?

The answers to these questions will determine the success or failure of your law firm.

So how will law firms know what really constitutes value to their clients? They will know by taking the following steps.

How to know what constitute value to your clients

Before commencing an engagement you need to know what the clients' expectations are. Why would they want to engage your firm to carry on the assignment? Without knowledge of the clients' expectations, it would be difficult to assess the outcome of your solution as valuable to them.

One reason why some professionals struggle to provide value is this. They are so good at solving problems; they jump headlong into a situation without first assessing the desired outcome. Baker explains it like this:

"Simply offering solutions to problems is not enough; the customer automatically expects problems to be solved, which is why they seek professional help in the first place...More emphasis needs to be placed on the total customer experience. Focusing on the total customer experience demonstrates not just competency but distinction".

To determine the expected outcome which translates into client value, clients should be asked the following questions.

- What are your expectations for this engagement?
- What work or business do you do?
- What are your critical success factors?
- How would this engagement add value to your life?
- Which of our offerings is of the highest value to you?
- What alternatives do you have in mind presently?
- What issues are you currently confronting in relation to your business that keeps you awake at night?
- How can this engagement help you eliminate those issues?
- What standard of service do you expect from us?

- What difference would our service make to your, productivity, profit, and results?
- How important is it to you for us to quickly respond to your queries?
- What would you consider to be a quick response to your queries?
- Why did you decide to change law firm?
- Why did you choose your previous law firm?
- What magazines and newspapers do you read?
- How would you define success after this engagement?

Of course use of any or all of these questions will depend on the type of client you are dealing with. However, they provide you with a template of the types of questions you would want to ask before preparing an engagement plan for a client.

There are two reasons for this:

- You get to know who your clients are so that you have an idea who your customer avatar is
- You get to decide the right engagement plan to sell to them

The above questions are pretty extensive, so of course they will be subject to the type of client you are engaged with. However, they do provide you with a template of the types of question you would want to ask before accepting any formal engagement.

The Strategic Pricing Strategy Canvas – How to use pricing to create new market

Ed Kless says *"If you suck at what you do, by all means price by the hour."*

Legal fees is one of the main bone of contention between lawyers and their clients as evident by my story and that of Duncan Bannatyne. Lawyers are used to charging by the hour. In the perception of most lawyers, they are paid for the time they spend on a particular engagement. This is an opaque way of thinking that has been difficult to erase from the legal profession.

Earlier I told the story of a consultant who I engaged to carry out some marketing research for me. When he presented his report I refused to pay him. Why? In my view he had not produced my desired result. He took legal action and in court presented a time sheet with the hours he spent on the job. The fact that he did not achieve my desired result was not an issue to him, the time he spent doing the job was more important to him.

It is my hope that every lawyer who reads this book would understand that it is not about the amount of hours you spent on a job, but the result that you produce for the client that matters. If you want to succeed in the 21st century legal business environment, your ability to differentiate your law firm through value pricing, will be the key that unlock your potential and create an unbelievable rush of new clients.

To quote Adam Smith again *"both the buyer and the seller must advance from an exchange, or it will not take place".*

Before starting any engagement, to ensure that the engagement is priced in such a way that it is profitable to both parties, you need to address two key questions:

- What outcome does the client seek for engaging our firm?
- How can we provide the service in a way that it is mutually beneficial to both parties?
- In other words, how much would it cost us to provide this service to the client that would make it profitable for both parties?

Why would most law firms focus on an hourly rate when charging clients? They do not go through their pricing process in this manner. If in your law firm you use the four steps below for strategically pricing your service prior to an engagement, you will stop charging hourly rates instead focus on the value you are providing the client. I can guarantee you that if you follow the four steps below, you will reap these benefits:

- Firstly, you will increase your profit margin per transaction.
- Secondly, you will significantly increase your number of new clients.

Step one – strategic pricing

- What would it cost clients in monetary terms if they engaged your firm?
- What in monetary value would the client gain from the engagement?
- What type of benefit would the client gain from the engagement?
- What value does the engagement bring to the client?
- How would the engagement move the client towards the achievement of his vision for the future?
- Does the engagement present any form of surprise to the client?

- How much does the competition charge for a similar service?
- Has the client ever gone to another law firm?
- How much does the client know about the solution they require?
- What level of tangible or intangible value would the client get from the solution?
- How much would the engagement cost the firm in terms of time and resources?
- What alternatives exist for your solution?
- Is the client aware of the alternatives?
- How can you reposition the solution in the mind of the client to make it more valuable to them?

I realise that if your law firm has not gone through this type of process in setting your prices, it could be a very difficult process. At times it might even feel unnecessary. However, what you need to appreciate is that the process is invaluable for creating the type of pricing strategy that will lead to substantial profit for your firm.

Step two – strategic pricing

Apply the principles of price discrimination.

Although you might provide two different clients the same type of service, the price might vary to each client depending on the amount of benefit each client receives from your service.

A common example of this might be public transport fares or gym membership. The cost of travelling at peak times is more than travelling at off peak times even though the travel destinations might be the same. If someone has a gym membership, the cost of going to the gym at peak times is different from the cost of going at off peak times.

Landsburg (1996) broke down price discrimination into three stages:

- First-degree price discrimination is when each client is charged the most that they are willing to pay for the service.
- Second-degree price discrimination is when the same client is charged a different price for identical items.
- Third-degree price discrimination occurs when a different price is charged in a different market.

As you work on your price, you will want to analyse your clients to ensure they are appropriately priced. Use price discrimination when necessary to ensure that your law firm derive profit commensurate with the amount of value you provide to clients.

Step three – strategic pricing

Charge for your service according to value and not per hour.

Let's imagine for a moment that we had to pay Einstein per hour for the time it took him to develop the "Theory of Relativity", or we had to pay Edison for coming up with the electric light; how much would we have had to pay them?

Not even the U.S. government would have been able to pay Einstein or Edison for their inventions. Malcolm Gladwell in his book entitled "Outliers" introduced the concept of the ten thousand hours. He said that in order to be proficient at any profession, one has to work at it for at least ten thousand hours. He went on to give examples of the likes of Bill Gates and Steve Jobs who spent the golden ten thousand hours on their trade before becoming excellent at it.

You have spent years to master your trade. You may have spent ten years in university and an additional five or ten years practicing. Do you really think that £200.00 or £300.00 per hour is what you are worth?

There is no amount you can place on Intellectual Capital (IC). When you buy a book from the bookstore it might cost you £20.00. However, if you got information from that book that made you a million pounds, would you say the book was worth £20.00? Here is an interesting question that I got from America's Business Philosopher Jim Rohn:

what would a book that saved you from a heart attack be worth to you? £20.00?

You undervalue yourself with hourly rates. When you set your charges based upon your hourly rate you feel that you are removing the risk from you and shifting it to the client. While this may be true, in the process, you also rob yourself of the chance to draw the appropriate value from your services. You are like a salesperson on salary. A salesperson could make a sale worth millions of pounds for his company, because he is on a fixed salary, he will receive only his monthly salary. At the same time his company might be basking in hundreds of thousands of pounds in profit from his sales.

There are times when your service can make an enormous difference to your clients' life. This is why you need to price your services strategically. You need to be prepared to absorb some of the risk and not to place all of the risk on the client. By absorbing some of the risk, you might end up not absorbing any risk at all because you will better be able to charge premium rate for your services.

Look at it as an insurance premium. You do pay insurance for your car, don't' you? You might not have an accident for five to ten years, yet every year you pay your insurance premium. Ever thought why? You believe in your mind that when you least expect it, you might have an accident and you will be better off covered.

The reality is, if you paid your insurance premium for ten years and you had an accident, will the insurance company lose anything by paying out for your accident? No. The money they will pay out might well be a fraction of the amount they collected from you over ten years.

The same will apply to you, when you know the value you are providing the client. By asking them the above questions, you are able to charge premium rates for your services. That is only possible because you would have established the value of your services in their minds.

I must repeat this point; you are not being paid for your time, you are being paid for the value you provide to the client.

Therefore if you provided a lot of value to the client, you should never feel guilty for charging a premium fee. When you provide more value than the amount you are paid, it means that you are working for free. That's how you need to see it.

There can never be a better time to be a professional. We are currently living in the 'Psychozoic Age,' the age of the mind. Wealth and opportunities are contained in your mind. The only limitation on the amount you can earn is the limitation you place on yourself. By focusing on your hourly rates, you are limiting the amount you can earn. I have personally purchased training programs valued at five thousand USD. I know of training programs that are valued at twenty-five thousand USD. Warrant Buffet paid Tony Robins seven million dollars for coaching. So you need to recognise that there are no limitations on how much you can earn from your IC as long as you provide value.

Steps For Creating A Value Pricing Canvas

Listed below are a few guides for value pricing your services to ensure you do not over charge clients and scare them away. They are also to ensure that you charge a fee that is profitable to your firm and conforms to the value of your service.

Step one – value pricing:

Focus on the value that you would provide to the client.

Thomas Nagle and Reed Holden (2002: 164) in "The Strategy and Tactics of Pricing" provides the five Cs. These are considerations you need to make about the value of your service to the client when setting your price.

- Comprehend value to the customers
- Create value for the customers
- Communicate the value you create
- Convince customers they must pay for the value
- Capture the value with strategic pricing based on value, not cost and effort.

By value pricing using the five Cs, you will be able to charge a premium rate for your services.

Clients would not complain, because they are able to understand the benefit to them.

Step two – value pricing:

Focus on the cost of the service to your firm.

In order to assess the cost of the service to your clients, you will need to apply a principle from project management concept called: the triple constraint – scope, resource and time of the project.

Scope: What outcome are you expecting at the end of the engagement? The outcome as I pointed out previously, needs to be sensor specific. There needs to be an evidence procedure for measuring the outcome of your solution.

Resources: How much resources would it require? The resources are manpower, finance and other elements of your firm's assets you will be expanding on the solution.

Time of engagement: how much time would it take to complete the engagement? Based upon experience of previous engagements you will be able to project the approximate length of time of the engagement.

Step three – value pricing:

Focus on the psychology of pricing

There is a saying in marketing, 'people buy emotionally but justify their decision logically.' The difference between a sale and a non-sale, also comes down to how the buyer feels about the person they are transacting with. When buyers like a seller they want to do business with that person. If buyers do not like the seller they do not feel comfortable and interaction is strained.

As you price your services, you need to be aware of buyers' psychology. Buyers buy for a reason other than value and quality. Understanding those other reasons will enable you to be able to strategically quote the right client the right price.

Ron Baker notes that there are two characteristics to price psychology; "Price Leverage and Price Emotions". He describes Price

Leverage as the question of who is the most price sensitive during negotiation. There are three types of Price Emotions which clients will experience during an interaction with your law firm. They are: price resistance, payment resistance and price anxiety. Clients are likely to experience the three of them during the negotiation. In his view, the best way of overcoming them is to focus on value rather than the price during negotiations. One way of ensuring this is through price bundling which focuses on the offering as a whole rather than on specific aspects.

Internet markets are the best at using price bundling. When internet information venders market their products, from the beginning of the sales process, they never mention anything about the price. They sometimes send ten to fifteen page sales letters. In the first thirteen pages they make no mention of the price of the products. All the prospect reads are the benefits of the product. And when they do mention the price, they don't just leave it hanging.

They give the price and then give a reason for it. Then maybe they offer a discount and give a reason why they are providing a discount. This is the reason why internet marketers are easily able to market information products worth thousands of pounds. They take their prospects' minds from the products and the price and focus it on the benefit they will derive from using the products.

The top pricing psychology used by the top internet marketers in the world is called; 'benefit within the benefit.' What is all this? It is based on the philosophy that there are two types of benefits that anyone can gain from using a product or service...the surface or direct benefit and the inner benefit or benefit within the benefit.

A good example of a benefit within benefit is a single woman going to buy a pair of stretched jeans for a date. Why does she want to buy stretched jeans for a date? So that her date would be able to view the full extent of her body shape. Why does she want him to be able to appreciate her body shape, to entice him to desire her even more. In this case, the benefit she gets from buying this pair of jeans is first and foremost the fact that she gets to have new jeans. In addition to the new jeans, she gets to have her date admire the shape or beauty of her body and desire her even more.

I use this example, in the hope it will clearly illustrate the point. So as you discuss the value of your firm's offering, and your pricing strategy, your focus need not be on the service itself or the immediate benefit the client will derive from it; it has to be on the ancillary benefits that might spring out as a result of the services you provide.

Step four – value pricing:

Focus on price sensitive clients:

To ascertain the reason behind client's price sensitivity, you will need to answer the following questions:

- Does the client know or believe that there is an alternative?
- Does the client perceive your offering to be so unique it is not available elsewhere?
- Can the client easily and cost-effectively go to another law firm?
- How informed is the client about competitive services?
- How convinced is the client that your price reflects the quality of your services?
- Does the client perceive your service as a high ticket item?
- In the eyes of your client, does the benefit of your service outweigh the cost of the service?
- Does the client perceive your price as fair and reasonable for the service?

Answers to these questions will provide you with clues as to why your client is price sensitive.

Step five – value pricing:

Focus on risk removal.

When clients are about to part with large sums of cash, their risk tolerance is considerably lower. This is why it is incumbent upon you when designing your pricing canvas you consider the clients' perception of risk and devise strategies for risk removal.

The following are a few of the risks clients might perceive:

- Delivery risk: your firm might not deliver on its promises
- Monetary risk: they might lose financially in the process
- Wasted time risk: they might lose unnecessary time in the process if your firm does not deliver as promised
- Emotional risk: the service might not be up to their expectations
- Social proof risk: the solution might not meet the approval of others and the mistake might demean them in the eyes of others
- Physical risk: the solution might actually cause physical harm to them.

As you design your pricing canvas, you need to consider all of the above perceived risks that might be going on in the minds of your clients and prepare an antidote to counter each of them.

Step six – value pricing:

Conduct an autopsy at the end of each engagement.

There are lessons to be learnt from each engagement in relation to your value pricing strategies. By going through an autopsy process, you will learn how you can increase your profit margin for future engagement while maximising the value to the client.

The process can be effectively conducted by answering the following questions:

- How much value did your firm add to your client after the engagement?
- Was it possible to add even more value to the client?
- If so what prevented your firm from adding the additional value to the client?
- What other extra services did you have to provide to the client?
- Was the price right?
- Was the client pleased with the price?
- Could you have charged a higher or lower price?
- How likely are you to get a referral from the client?
- How much value did your firm gain from the exercise?
- How much more would your firm have gained if you had provided a different solution?
- What was resources cost to your firm for this engagement?
- How would you conduct similar engagement in the future? If differently, How?
- What did you gain from the engagement in terms of learning and personal development?
- How much did your team learn from the engagement?
- How can you handle similar engagement better in the future?

Value innovation and strategic pricing will be the new competitive advantage in the legal profession. Law firms that grapple with this fact and begin to introduce them into their firm will be way ahead of the pack by the time other law firms wake up to it. 90% of businesses and individuals are unhappy with their law firms. What this means for your firm is that nine out of ten people that are right now using legal services can be your client. That is of course if you implement the strategies I have provided here.

You do not need some ingenious marketing strategy to acquire new clients to move your law firm from start-up to 7 Figure. All you need is to redefine value in terms of your client and stop focusing on hourly rates. You will attract more clients than you can handle. Moving a law firm from start-up to a 7 Figure operation is not an enigma; it just requires going against the grain and doing things differently.

Be a true professional: care about your clients. I mean really care about them. If you do, your law firm would grow beyond your wildest expectations.

Remember, "Blue Ocean" strategy is a dynamic process. Therefore, you should not rest on your laurels. You need to understand that competition is always around the corner. Also that, "Blue Ocean" strategy is not about redefining the problem in the industry; No. It is about finding solutions to existing problems which cannot be done by your competitors.

Philosopher Eric Hoffer in his book 'The Ordeal of Change,' speaks of change as a move from the old to the new. He said:

"The plunge into the new is often an escape from an untenable situation and a manoeuvre to mask one's ineptness. To adopt the role of the pioneer and avant-garde is to place oneself in a situation where ineptness and awkwardness are acceptable and even unavoidable".

You have a chance to take the plunge and break away from the pack. It is my hope that you 'carpe diem' – seize the opportunity.

Chapter Four: How to Recruit and Retain an 'A Talent'

Arsenal FC is an English football team. It is rated as one of the world's top football clubs and the third richest in the world. On a good day, Arsenal is capable of making football teams including the likes of Barcelona and Manchester United look ordinary.

But Arsenal FC has not won a trophy since the 2003-04 season. It had a glimpse of the top spot as runners-up in the UEFA 2005-06 Champions League. A year earlier in the 2003-04 English season it notched up a record when it became only the second club in the history of English football to complete a season without losing a game.

However, after the departure of key players in 2005 and 2007, the club's fortunes went into decline. Why would such a great football club lose its winning ways?

Answer: It is short of 'A talents'. When Arsenal was on top, it was bolstered by imported players, most of them members of foreign national teams. A player must be an 'A talent' to play for his country.

The best football clubs in the world attract the best players in the world. Barcelona considered the best club in the world has five of the world's top football players. When the Spanish National Team won the FIFA World Cup in South Africa, they had eight of the world's best football players.

Every winning sport team has a handful of 'A talents' that serves as the hub around which the rest of the team plays. When Brazil won the FIFA World Cup, they had Pele as the point man and in later years Romário. When France won the FIFA World Cup, Zidane was the glue that held the team together. Barcelona without Messi will not remain the best team in the world for a long time. In basketball you have the likes of Michael Jordan, Kobe Bryant or LeBron James who serve as the glue to hold their teams together.

I have used a football team as a case study to commence a chapter in a business book on how to recruit 'A talents' because the dynamics at play in the world of football are also at play in the world of business. There could hardly be a better example to illustrate the importance of 'A talents'.

If your goal is to move your legal firm from start-up to 7 Figure, the first port of call needs to be the recruitment of 'A talents'. *"In fact, leaders of companies that go from good to great"* Jim Collins said *"start not with where but with whom."* They start by getting the right people on the bus, the wrong people off and the right people in the right seats. They stick with that discipline—first the people, then the direction—no matter how dire the circumstances".

However, an 'A talent' is not easy to find. He does not go to the Job Centre on Monday morning to look for a job; neither does he scan job vacancies in newspapers. In fact he is already employed. An 'A talent' who is unemployed is either not an 'A talent' or he is unemployed by choice. But you will not want to bank on that because in 99.9% of the cases your 'A Talent' is already employed or running his own show.

The question I hear you asking is; if they are already employed, how can a legal firm seeking to add to its team find 'A talents'? The answer is simple. You need to scout and poach them just as sports teams do. All 'A talents' are ambitious people. They are always seeking new challenges. Your job if you want to recruit them is to convince them that your legal firm provides a challenging opportunity.

Here are four principles for recruiting 'A talents':

1. You should be an 'A talent' yourself (in order to sell your accounting firm to them)

2. You need to create a conducive work environment

3. You need to create good systems

4. You need to have metric for measuring staff performance

Why You Need An 'A Talent' On Your Team

Bill Gates – *"Take our best 20 people away, and I will tell you that Microsoft would become an unimportant company."*

Bear in mind Microsoft has close to half a million employees, yet Mr Gates believes that if only 20 are removed from the company, the company will become irrelevant.

This statement confirms my earlier assertion in the football scenario, that 'A talents' are the key to organisational success. Check out any successful company, you will find a handful of 'A talents' in the driving seat of the company.

In his book Top Grading, author Brad Smart outlined the following as a few of the benefits of hiring 'A talents':

- Paper plant managed by A's has a 94 per cent higher profit than other paper plants.
- More talent investment banking associates are twice as productive as those average in talent.
- Return to shareholders for companies with top talent practices averages 22 per cent above industry means.
- The top 3 per cent of programmers produce 1,200 per cent more lines of code than the average; the top 20 per cent produce 320 per cent more than the average.
- The top 3 per cent of salespeople produce up to 250 per cent more than average; the top 20 per cent produce up to 120 per cent more".

This is one of the instances in human activities that the 80/20 principle is more prevalent. The only difference is that in this instance, it is more like 97/3. The top three to five per cent of employees in any organisation produce more than the remaining 97 per cent. Your challenge as an entrepreneur lawyer is to figure out ways of hiring employees that belong to the three per cent because it takes just one of those employees to change your legal firm.

To paraphrase Brad Smart once again; 'A talents' contribute more; are more innovative; work smarter; are more trustworthy and resourceful; take more initiative; develop better business strategies; articulate their vision clearly; deliver higher quality; work efficiently and effectively; work better as a member of a team; completes tasks and can attract other 'A talents'.

Let's now examine what are the effects of not having 'A talents' in an organisation.

The Cost Of Hiring The Wrong Talent

The cost of hiring the wrong talent can be enormous for small to medium size legal firms. Here I will again use the football analogy for lack of a better and more explicit example.

Football is a big business in Europe. Advancing in international competitions can result in handsome rewards for clubs both in ticket sales and payment from the football governing bodies. Therefore, clubs fight tooth and nail to ensure they secure a European spot each and every season. And the further a club advance in European competition, the more money the team makes that season. The bottom clubs of most European leagues continue to struggle because they have not had the chance of playing in Europe therefore do not have the resources to buy the types of players that will help them advance in Europe.

The situation with the football is like "chicken and egg". A club needs to win trophies or at least play in European Championship to boost its finances. But as they go after 'A talent,' some clubs end up spending millions on good players.

Hardly a season goes by without high profile signings. In their desperate effort to acquire good players, clubs end up spending millions that they cannot afford to buy good players but when those players come they end up becoming a disappointment. This might not be entirely the players' fault because in order for an "A talent" to flourish, there need to be other things in place.

A few high profile signings that immediately come to mind are Chelsea's signing of Andriy Shevchenko for £30 million, he played only a few games for the club and had to be let go off. Chelsea signing of Fernando Torres from Liverpool for £50 million has been a complete disaster with him scoring only a single goal for his first season. And then there is Manchester City signing of Carlos Tevez paying him a quarter of a million pound a week only for him to leave for his country to play golf while he is still being paid his weekly wages. However, such 'mis-hiring' as it is known is not only limited to football clubs or sport. In fact it might even be more prevalent in the corporate world.

According to a 2004 study, the average cost of mis-hiring of mid-managers with the base salary of £100,000 is fifteen times their base salary or £1.5 million per mis-hire.

The cost was calculated using the following criteria:

- Cost of hiring £31,643
- Cost of compensation (all year) £255,452
- Cost of maintaining a person in a job £67,653
- Severance £33,962
- Cost of mistake, failure, wasted and missed business opportunity £1,232,092
- Cost of disruption £242,356
- Sum up costs £1,863,158
- Value of contribution £360,721
- Net average cost of mis-hire £1,502,436

(Source B. Smart: Top Grading)

If your legal firm uses these calculations as a template for calculating your mis-hiring it would help you come to terms with the benefit of hiring "A talents".

As an entrepreneur lawyer who wants to move your legal firm from start-up to 7 Figure, you cannot afford to make such costly mistakes. Hence the reason why it is important that you hire only 'A talents' and that you have a process in place for ensuring you attract 'A talents' to your practice.

Let's now breakdown each of the four principles for employing 'A talents'

- You have to be an "A talent" yourself in order to sell your practice to them
- You need to create a conducive work environment
- You need to create good systems
- You need to have metrics for measuring staff performance

How to Become an 'A talent'

"To attract attractive people you need to be attractive", America's business philosopher Jim Rohn, said.

At one point in my business, I felt I needed a sales and marketing manager. I placed a job ad for the position and I received lots of responses. I filtered the applications and invited only the best ones for interview. What I noticed was that whenever, I interviewed a very good candidate who I was excited about and really wanted to employ, the person never accepted my offer of employment.

I ended up employing the second or third choice candidate who I had to get rid of after a few months because they turned out to be unsuitable for the job. I could not figure out why the best candidates did not want to work for me until I got into consultancy and read 'Top-grading' by Brad Smart. Top-grading opened my eyes. 'A talents' shy away from working with anything but 'A talents.'

When 'A talents' came to me for an interview, they sensed that I was not an 'A talent' and as such did not want to work with or for me.

Steps for becoming an 'A talent':

Step one – Identify your talent

Who are 'A talents'?

- They are the best of the best in the class. They are the rare species of the human race who are able to create the extraordinary from the ordinary.
- They are the entrepreneurs who change our lives with a single idea.
- They are the scientists who discovered cancer treatment and they are researchers through whose research HIV sufferers can live longer.

- They are Olympic gold medallist and the athletes from poor nations who despite the odds make it to the Olympics and win the gold medal.
- They are baseball players who can hit a home run at crucial points of the game.
- They are football players who score world cup winning goals.
- They are charity workers working to make a difference in the most remote villages at the end of the earth.
- They are those with the ability to take your legal firm from start-up to 7 Figure in twelve months. They are special and rare, and they make up only a fraction of our population. But they make more impact than the majority 97 per cent.

So what is your talent? What ordinary thing can you do extraordinarily well? That is your talent.

Step two – Identify your strength

What is strength?

In his book "Now Discover Your Strengths" author Marcus Buckingham describes strength as a *"consistent near perfect performance in any activity"*. He said that by defining strength in this manner, we focus on three characteristics.

- Engagement in certain activities consistently
- Realisation that you do not need to be strong in every aspect of your role in order to excel
- You can excel only by maximising your strength

It is your talent, knowledge and skill that combine to create your strength.

Based on this simple definition: *"consistent near perfect performance in any activity"* what do you consider your strength?

What can you do near perfectly?

That is your strength. In order to become an 'A talent' you need to be able to identify your strengths and increase your ability to maximise them.

Your talent is your natural patterns of thoughts, feeling and behaviour. However, in order to maximise the use of your talent, you need to develop it by constant usage.

England's David Beckham is a natural free kick specialist. However, he worked for hours each day on his kicking abilities to constantly remain at the top of his game.

England's Rugby star Jonny Wilkinson spent hours each day working on his kicking abilities despite the fact that he was the best at it in the world of Rugby.

Steve Jobs arguably the best salesman who ever lived used to practice each of his presentations for weeks on end prior to the release of each Apple product.

When we see high performers in action, there is the tendency to assume that they are just blessed with extraordinary talents. Yes, it might be true that they are gifted. However, in order to perform at a high level and remain at the top of their game they must constantly practice. You don't learn to ride a bicycle at a weekend seminar, you need to actually get on a bicycle and ride.

It is easy to improve your knowledge these days. With the amount of information available, the problem you are faced with is not the lack of information with which to increase your knowledge and skills, but your ability to absorb the available information.

Let me make the distinction between learning for the sake of learning and just-in-time learning. With the plethora of information available at the touch of a button today; you need to ensure that the knowledge you gain, is just-in-time. That is the information that is necessary for you to be able to perform. You need to identify your learning objectives, clarify the skills set needed to achieve those objectives and focus your learning by acquiring those skills relating to your learning objectives. That is just-in-time learning.

> The extent to which you are able to structure your work will be the level to which you will be able to increase your knowledge and skills level. The outcome of any work related activity is either to remove a constraint or improve a situation. To accomplish either of these, you will need to focus on productivity instead of activity; and personal effectiveness instead of efficiency.

You need efficiency in order to ensure the activities are carried out in the most cost-effective manner and within a reasonable timescale. But you need effectiveness to produce results. Therefore in order to produce the desired results; it is imperative that you increase your knowledge and skills level.

So to become an 'A talent', you need to identify your strength: talent, knowledge and skill and work on increasing those related to your activities and desired objectives.

Step three – Identify your objective

What is your outcome?

The third step in the process of becoming an 'A talent' is the ability to clearly define your objective and outcome for any activity you are engaged in.

One of the skills that 'A talents' possess that others don't, are their ability to focus on the task at hand. They achieve that by setting clear objectives and outcomes for their activities. It is impossible to hit a target you cannot see. Therefore, in order to hit a target, you have to first create the target. To become an 'A talent' it is imperative that you are capable of setting clear objective and outcomes for activities you are engaged in.

Let me end this section with The Peter Principle. I believe it is very appropriate for our topic of discussion.

> *"The Peter Principle states that "in a hierarchy every employee tends to rise to his level of incompetence." This means that employees tend to be promoted until they reach a position in which they cannot work competently…The principle holds that in a hierarchy, members are promoted so long as they work competently. Eventually they are promoted to a position in which they are no longer competent (their "level of incompetence"), and there they remain unable to earn further promotions"*

The general consensus amongst most entrepreneur lawyers is that business is common sense. They feel all they need is to learn is law and when it comes to the business of law they can wing it. That perception is wrong.

Business is not common sense. To create a multi-billion pound business from scratch often requires a kind of specialized knowledge which common sense lacks.

Apple is more valuable than the U.S. government. Just in case you needed reminding the U.S. is the most powerful nation on earth and Apple is more valuable in monetary terms than the U.S. government. To build a business from the ground to become more valuable than the most powerful nation on earth does not just require common sense.

When you speak or listen to people who have achieved extraordinary success, you come to the realisation that those people did not just succeed because they had more common sense than the rest of humanity, they have strength and skills that the majority of people lack.

To move a legal firm from start-up to 7 Figure requires strength and skills that an average entrepreneur lawyer lacks. There are lots of lawyers who have succeeded in creating extraordinary legal firms from scratch. But thousands of legal firms have gone out of business or struggle to survive. All had common sense but those who made a success of their business also had strength and specialised skills to do so.

When you develop your skill and strength you can move your legal firm into the 7 Figure business within twelve months. When you become an 'A talent' you are able to attract 'A talents' who are ready to help you move your firm to a 7 Figure business.

Where to find 'A talents'

Your competition

There is bad news and good news about finding 'A talents.' The bad is as I previously intimated, 'A talents' are only about three to five per cent of the human race. Furthermore, they are all presently employed by your competitors or are running their own businesses. All the best CEOs, football managers and coaches are employed, if they were not, that would be a reason for concern.

The good news is that 'A talents' are not mercenaries; they do not work for the highest bidder. They are ambitious, passionate and love challenges. They want to make a difference to their community and the world. That is why as an entrepreneur lawyer your vision for your legal firm needs to be great. It does not matter how small your legal firm may be at present, if you have a large enough vision, you can still lure 'A talents' to your team.

There is this famous story of Steve Jobs and John Sculley who was a Pepsi executive. When Jobs wanted to lure him to Apple the question that Jobs asked him was:

> *"Do you want to sell sugar water for the rest of your life, or do you want to come with me and change the world"?*

Even though Pepsi is a global brand, far bigger than Apple, Jobs was able to poach him from Pepsi with a vision of changing the world.

Therefore you must realise firstly that 'A talents' are employed but they can be poached from your competitors with the right amount of incentive. At the end of every season, sport teams trade players. An 'A talent' might be playing for one team; he could be either dissatisfied or he might just be looking for a new challenge. A footballer may want to win the Champions League or they may want to have more playing time because their current club is made up of many other 'A talents', therefore he might not have the amount of playing time he would like. There is always a good reason why an 'A talent' might want to move. All you need to do is give them that reason.

Events

Another place to find an 'A talent' is at professional gatherings, conferences, training workshops, trade shows and networking events. People attend all of these events for their own reasons that might not be in compliance with their company's objectives. As an entrepreneur lawyer, you need to have the mind-set of a constant recruiter. When you engage in conversation with people at those events, you need to keep your antennas up for any trace of an 'A talent'. The moment you notice one, try to strike a conversation with the individual and find out as much as you can about them.

Collect their details, stay in touch and let them know that you are always on the lookout for 'A talents'. Tell them things like: if they ever wanted a career change they should consider contacting you.

Your contacts

You can also find an 'A talent' through your own network:

- your family and friends
- neighbour
- acquaintances

Social media

Social media will have a useful part to play in your search for 'A talents'. So make full use of your contacts on Facebook, Twitter, Google plus and Linkedin. But be very careful. Do not trust posted profiles and never use them as a base from which to make judgement about appropriateness of a candidate for your legal firm.

Recruitment Agencies

Recruitment agencies usually have a database of 'A talents'.

The first rule of thumb here is: it needs to be a head-hunter not a conventional recruitment agency.

Secondly, you need to have evidence that the agency concerned has a penchant for and a background for recruiting 'A talents.'

Thirdly, the person handling your requirements has to be an 'A talent.' Remember 'A talents' don't work for 'B or C talents'.

Daily contacts

People you interact with during the course of your day. You might interact with sales people, receptionists and other professionals. You need to make it a habit of talking to such people as they might be looking for a change. For example, you have a brilliant sales person who sold you something. He might be looking for a change. Sound him out. As an entrepreneur lawyer, you interact with supply companies. You interact with other lawyers and staff from other legal firms. If they as much as appear to be 'A talents' strike up the conversation. Feel them out.

Current employees

Your current 'A talent' employees might know other 'A talents'. They may be their friends, even family! Remember the old saying birds of the same feather flock together. Give them incentives for introducing you to other 'A talents' like themselves.

Create a Conducive Working Environment

Jim Rohn's quotation is also very relevant for this section:

"to attract attractive people you need to be attractive".

As an employer, you are also marketing your organisation to applicants. Like you, they are apprehensive; they are asking themselves whether joining your legal firm would be a good decision. You often see that in sports; where high profile 'A talent' might be courted by several different clubs at the same time. The player has to make a decision as to which club to join. Sometimes it can be an agonising decision as all the top clubs might be presenting him with similar offers. When players are faced with such predicament, it sometimes comes down to the working environment...the history of the club, the stadium and the fans.

This scenario is also at play when you try to lure an 'A talent' to your legal firm. As most lawyers know, the dream of almost all legal graduates is to work for big legal firms where they will have access to fancy technologies and good benefits. Therefore if you aim to entice them to work for your legal firm, you need to create a good working environment.

I will use the Arsenal situation as an example again. Arsenal is a very ambitious club. They aim to win trophies as they have done previously. Big problem, they cannot attract the type of players that will help them achieve the level of success they require. Reason: they are the only club in England that officially has a wage cap.

Football is a big business. Premiership players are now earning as high as £250.000 per week. Football players themselves are becoming savvy. They know their worth therefore, will not settle for less. By sticking to their policy of wage cap, Arsenal is robbing itself of the types of players it needs to achieve its ambition. Many of their best players are leaving the club because of the wage cap.

When Manchester City Football club was bought by Sheikh Mansour bin Zayed Al Nahyan, he sat his ambition on winning the Premier League. He understood that with the manager and players the club had at the time it would have been impossible to achieve that vision. Therefore, he went about changing the manager and bought some 'B+ and B Talent' players who have changed the fortune of the club. As I write this book, they are at the top of the Premier League plus they are still in Europe.

There are two important lessons to be learnt from the two above examples. The first lesson is: you have the team Arsenal that wants to achieve greatness but is not prepared to create the environment to attract the types of players that would help it achieve greatness.

Secondly, there is Manchester City FC that sets its eyes on greatness and is creating the type of environment that would allow it to achieve its goals. But notice something I said about Manchester City FC, I said they managed to attract 'B+ and B talents'. Even though they are willing to pay for 'A talents', 'A talents' do not want to play for the club because they have no history of success?

They have no result that will demonstrate to 'A talents' that they can achieve what they set out to achieve. After a few seasons when they might have won the Premiership, then they will be able to attract some 'A talents'.

This is a very crucial point I would like you to pay attention to. 'A talents' want the things that come with success, but they are not mercenaries, they cannot be bought by the highest bidder. They need more than just money, they need tangible evidence that the organisation concern will achieve its goals. Manchester City FC has not won a trophy in over 40 years and everyone knows that building a winning team takes time. Therefore for now Manchester City FC is not attractive enough to attract 'A talents'.

To attract 'A talent' you first need to create the environment in which they will flourish. There needs to be evident procedure to demonstrate your determination to achieve your vision. This is the reason why in the first instant I said you need to become an 'A talent' yourself. If they see that you are an 'A talent' and they believe in your capability, they might take the risk of joining your legal firm.

How to recruit 'A talents'

Is the process for recruiting an 'A talent' an art or a science? I will argue that it is both. On the art side there is the use of intuition, instinct and judgement to make a pronouncement on someone you might be meeting for the first time. The ability to effectively analyse another human being is not an exact science. We know fully well that human beings are complex and complicated creatures that evolve as the situation demands.

The science of the process involves putting in place mechanisms that ensure the procedure is less subjective. The aim of this section is to provide you with the tools for ensuring that your process of recruitment is not riddled with subjectivity and sentiment. Recruitment is not an exact science. It is a process riddled with our own biases. However, by institutionalising certain measures, there is the possibility of reducing sentiment from the process.

There are a few principles which are necessary for ensuring an effective recruitment process...

'A talent' recruitment principle 101: always be recruiting

As an entrepreneur, you should always be on the lookout for 'A talents'. Whenever you notice them, grab them straight away. That could mean the difference between success and failure for your legal firm.

> Margaret Mead makes this point even better when she says "Never doubt that a small group of committed people can change the world. Indeed it is the only thing that ever has."

I will also take a leaf from Jim Collins' "Good to Great" to better illustrate this point:

> *"Consider the case of Wells Fargo. Wells Fargo began its fifteen-years tint of spectacular performance in 1983, but the foundation for the shift dates back to the early 1970s, when then-CEO Dick Cooley began building one of the most talented management teams in the industry (the best team, according to investor Warren Buffett). Cooley foresaw that the banking industry would eventually undergo wrenching changes, but he did not pretend to know what form that change would take. So instead of mapping out a strategy for change, he and chairman Ernie Arbuckle focused on "injecting an endless stream of talent" directly into the veins of the company. They hired outstanding people whenever and wherever they found them, often without any specific job in mind. "That's how you build the future," he said. "If I'm not smart enough to see the changes that are coming, they will. And they'll be flexible enough to deal with them."* Cooley's approach proved prescient. No one could predict all the changes that would be wrought by banking deregulation. Yet when these changes came, no bank handled those chal-

lenges better than Wells Fargo. At a time when its sector of the banking industry fell 59 per cent behind the general stock market, Wells Fargo outperformed the market by over three times.

Carl Reichardt, who became CEO in 1983, attributed the banks success largely to the people around him, most of whom he inherited from Cooley. He listed members of the Wells Fargo executive team that had joined the company during the Cooley-Reichardt era, we were stunned. Nearly every person had gone on to become CEO of a major company.

One of the key components responsible for turning HP into a global brand was the ingenious people decision the company made after the second world war. When companies were laying-off workers, HP took the opportunity to recruit the best engineers and scientists in the country. That decision to recruit the best brains at the time was responsible for propelling HP to world dominance. When those people began producing dividends, they placed HP way ahead of the competition.

Always remember that an 'A talent' is never a liability, they are an investment.

'A talent' recruitment principle 102: recruit to meet a specific objective

In order to grow from your current stage to become a 7 Figure per annum legal firm, you will need to recruit people to fill specific positions in your practice in relation to your expansion plan.

This might appear to be a contradiction between this section and the one that preceded it. In the preceding section I said that you should always be recruiting 'A talents;' now I am saying you should recruit to fill specific needs.

I will clarify this point in two parts:

Part One

The more 'A talents' you have, the faster your organisation will grow.

> **David Parker** – the co-founder of HP stated that *"No company can grow revenues consistently faster than its ability to get enough of the right people to implement that growth and still become a great company. If your growth rate in revenues consistently outpaces your growth rate in people, you simply will not-indeed - build a great company".*

'A talent' has the vision to see further ahead; therefore the ability to make good future orientated decisions. This is a very important point that should not be underestimated. As Jim Collins pointed out, this was one of the factors responsible for propelling companies from good to great. According to Mr Collins, the companies that made the leap from good to great got more of their decisions right than their competitors who failed to make the leap.

To use the football analogy again, the difference between a star striker and a mediocre one is the ability to make the right decision in front on the goal. While the star striker might hit the target 50% of the time, the mediocre striker might hit the target only about two per cent of the time. The right decision at the right moment can change the future of your firm.

Part Two

Your recruitment has to be in alignment with your goals. As you create your vision for your legal firm, it is essential that you map out the type and number of people you will need to achieve that vision. Once you have an avatar of the type of people who you believe can help you to achieve your vision. You need to set out to attract those people as a part of your recruitment objectives and expansion plan. Every person you recruit has to be with the expressed purpose of filling a position that relates directly to your growth plan. Those who transform a legal firm from start-up to 7 Figure are not just ordinary people; they are 'A talents' with the ability to do extraordinary things.

'A talent' recruitment principle 103: do not settle, take as long as it is necessary to find the right candidate.

Peter Drukker once stated that:

"The ability to make good decisions regarding people represents one of the last reliable sources of competitive advantage, since very few organizations are good at it"

The legendary Jack Welch added:

"Nothing matters more in winning than getting the right people on the field. All the clever strategies and advanced technologies in the world are not effective without great people to put them to work"

The importance of hiring the right people was highlighted further by Jim Collins:

He gave the following example…

But how many executives have the discipline of David Maxwell, who held off on completing a developing a strategy until he got the right people in place. And that while the company was losing $1 million every single business day with $56 billion of loans underwater? When Maxwell became CEO of Fannie Mae during its darkest days, the board desperately wanted to know how he was going to rescue the company. Despite the immense pressure to act, to do something dramatic, to seize the wheel and start driving, Maxwell focused first on getting the right people on the Fannie Mae management team... Dick Cooley and David Maxwell both exemplified a classic Level 5 style when they said, *"I don't know where we should take this company, but I do know that if I start with the right people, ask them the right questions, and engage them in vigorous debate, we will find a way to make this company great."* ...When Colman Mockler became CEO of Gillette, he didn't go on a rampage, want only throwing people out the windows of a moving bus. Instead, he spent fully 55 per cent of his time during his first two years in office jiggering around with the management team, changing or moving thirty-eight of the top fifty people. According to Mockler, *"Every minute devoted to putting the proper person in the proper slot is worth weeks of time later".*

The organisations that made the leap from Good to Great understood this point very well. Good strategy and technology are essential for achieving greatness. But without the right people to implement those strategies, it is impossible for an organisation to attain greatness.

As you embark on your search for the right people, be aware that it is not going to be easy because the 95/5% rule also applies to recruitment. What this means is that 95% of applicants for a vacant position are not going to be the right people for the job. Only five per cent of your job applicants will be suitable for the position. Your job would be to weed out the five per cent from the lot. That is not an easy task.

Since coming to the UK and living in the UK for a while, I have been able to develop a theory about the workforce in the UK. My theory is this: one – three – ninety-one.

What this means is that one per cent of the people who live in the UK are the best in the world at what they do. Three per cent are equally as good as the best people anywhere in the world and the ninety-one per cent are, well, mediocre.

The obvious question is if only four per cent of the people in the UK are good at what they do, how come the country is still functioning? The answer is simple: the four per cent are so good; they carry the rest of the country along.

It is the BBC, J.K. Rowling, Judi Dench, the British Army, James Bond and The Economist, these individuals and institutions are so good that they carry the rest of the country with them.

This theory should not be a surprise to anyone who is familiar with the 80/20 or 95/5 rule. In most areas of life, this theory holds true. In sport for example all sport teams will have one or two players who are the heart of the team. Without them the team cannot perform to its optimal. Only about five per cent of the people in every business are responsible for 95% of the profit.

I introduced these points to further emphasize the importance of not settling until you find the right people. The right people can change your legal firm and help you achieve your goals. But you need to have the discipline to wait. Do not compromise. Find them.

Systems and Metric for performance measurement

The importance of systems have already been dealt with in chapter one. Productivity metrics and metrics for measuring employee performance will be addressed in detail in chapter six. However, I want to briefly point out again that 'A talent' will not flourish in an organisation that is chaotic. They thrive better in an organisation that has systems and work performance measurement mechanisms in place.

When an employee performance measurement system is in place, it allows 'A talents' staff to assess their performance against the company's benchmark. That way, employees can always see whether they meet or exceed job expectations.

Below is a list of steps recommended by Brad Smart in his book 'Top-Grading' on how to recruit "A talents"…

- Conduct thorough analysis of applicant's CV
- Generate a Candidate Assessment Scorecard (CAS) after analyzing the applicant's CV.
- Conduct thorough career assessment from the first job they ever had in their life. You may go as far as temporary job while in college
- Initiate and conduct telephone interview
- Conduct a five to seven hour competency interview spread across several visits
- Observe their informal interaction during those visits
- Conduct another interview, preferably another two interviews
- HR conduct a preliminary record check
- You or another senior staff conduct a second record check
- Prepare a written report of the process.

Adhere to Mr. Smart's recommended recruitment process. This is not always an easy endeavour for any organisation let alone a small legal firm. However, what needs to be considered is that the cost of mis-hiring can be expensive. Therefore, it is very important that the right candidate is recruited in the first instance. But to ensure that the right candidate is recruited, the process has to be thorough. As a small legal firm, you might not even have an HR department. If that is the case, you need to ensure that you personally supervise the process to ensure that all the above steps are followed and adhered to.

Chapter Five: How to gain Work-life Balance as a Lawyer

Mihaly Csikszentmihalyi in his book 'Flow; describes flow as *"a state of concentration or complete absorption with the activity at hand and the situation".* Furthermore he clarified it as; *"a state in which people are so involved in an activity that nothing else seems to matter."* (Csikszentmihalyi, 1990).

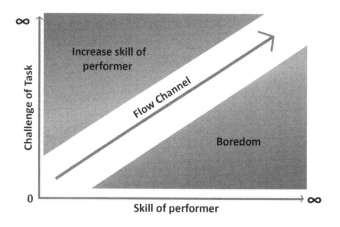

The achievement of 'flow' requires a balance between the challenge of a task and the skill of the performer. If the task is too easy the person would experience boredom in contrary if the task is too difficult, the individual will have to raise his skill level to match the task or may not experience 'flow'.

> *"Repression is not the way to virtue,"* Csikszentmihalyi said; *"when people restrain themselves out of fear, their lives are by necessity diminished. Only through freely chosen discipline can life be enjoyed and still kept within the bounds of reason."*

I once watched a Csikszentmihalyi presentation. He revealed that when he was a boy in his native Hungary during the Second World War, he witnessed how some adults coped with difficult situations in the midst of a state of hopelessness. He said some people had lost their entire livelihood, yet they lived happy lives.

Why Lawyers are not Achieving Work-life Balance

As I listened I was struck by this comment. It occurred to me that professionals decades ago took a lot of time and effort to accomplish certain tasks. Today those same tasks that would have taken hours to complete can be completed in minutes; yet professionals today struggle to achieve work-life balance.

As a lawyer, think of what your colleagues needed to do two or three decades ago to accomplish a simple task for a client. Can you imagine how far the legal profession have come?

As far as I can recall, the hours of the day have not changed from the last few decades. Decades ago when lawyers needed to physically perform a task for their clients, there were 24 hours in a day. With the advancement in technology that makes it possible for tasks to be easily performed remotely, there are still 24 hours in a day. Therefore, I am a bit perplexed as to why a lawyer still does not have enough time to create work-life balance.

> As professionals with your Blackberries and Tablets, you can literally take your office out with you so you have the ability to accomplish tasks on the go. You now have automated babysitters called television and video games to occupy your children. So what have you done with the extra time?

Think about it.

And you are not as wealthy as, or wealthier than lawyers of decades ago. Your standard of living may have changed but when you factor in inflation against what you earn these days, you are still earning the same amount or even less than lawyers who did not have access to technology.

So why is it that with all the advances in technology you still struggle to find time to spend with your loved ones or for extra-curricular activities?

The answer is decidedly simple; the large majority of you do not have 'flow' in your lives and you lack the ability to self-manage.

'Flow' as I pointed out is the state in which your skill level matches the activities you are engaged in. Skill in this sense does not mean legal training that you acquired in law school. The skill you are lacking is the skill to manage yourself and work effectively.

Almost every lawyer struggles with work-life balance. The higher you get in your career the higher the demand on your time and expertise. Conventional wisdom holds that the harder we work, the better our career prospects, consequently as you progress in your career you work harder and harder.

The hardest of all workers are professional entrepreneurs such as you: lawyers, accountants, dentists and consultants who are already used to working hard. As an entrepreneur lawyer, you tend to work twice as hard as you worked when you were employed. In this instant you are no longer just an employee you are now an employer and an owner.

This again comes down to the conventional belief that entrepreneurs have to work harder from the start. The logic is that to get your business off the ground, in the first few years you have to put in the hours. While it is true that getting a business off the ground requires long hours of hard work, it does not necessarily mean that all the hard work has to be done by the entrepreneur.

Secondly, putting in long hours of hard work is not guaranteed to make a business venture successful. Success or failure has little or nothing to do with the amount of labour of love that you put in. It has everything to do with the four plus one fundamental elements of a successful business outlined in chapter one.

In order to achieve work-life balance, you will need to apply three of those elements to your life.

Self-Management Not Time Management

There are some issues regarding work-life balance that needs outlining before going on to the core components:

1. Forget everything you were taught in school, they do not apply to entrepreneurship – Successful entrepreneurship is about doing the counterintuitive. The structured and intuitive stuff you were taught in school does not work in entrepreneurship. If you ever try applying the intuitive stuff you learnt during your professional training to your new role as an entrepreneur you are going to fail woefully.

2. It is not about you, but about it – In most instances, entrepreneurs try to handle everything on their own; they do not seek help because they truly believe that they do not need help. As a leader, it is no longer about you. It is no longer about your ability or inability to handle things on your own, it is about the mission, the goal and the good of the business as an entity.

3. You can never manage time but you can manage yourself
– Stephen Covey once said "Time management is a misnomer
the challenge is to manage ourselves". Most professionals attend time management seminars to learn how to manage
their time when what really needs managing is themselves.
There are 24 hours in a day; that will never change. Therefore,
the trick is to avoid overloading your day and focus instead
on maximising your productivity in those 24 hours. The basic
tenet of this principle is this; it is not about how many hours
you work but how much you get done in the hours you work.

**4. Your level of performance on a given day is a function of
your mental state** – This principle highlights a very important
aspect of productivity. That is, your level of productivity is
the function of your state of mind. As humans, when we are
stressed and tired our ability to produce results is considerably diminished. Most lawyers are always in what Tony
Schwartz the author of "The Power of Full Engagement" describes as the "grey zone"; working below your full capacity.
This is directly related to your mental state while at work. In
sport there is the saying that it is 90% mental.

5. 80% of what you do results in only 20% of your results –
The 80/20 or 95/5 rule is a very important phenomenon for
achieving work-life balance. The reality is 95% of your activities only result in five per cent of the results you produce and
five per cent of your activities result in 95% of your results.
Think about that!

You do not have infinite time. Time is finite. This means that
in order for you to be able to fit the important things into
your day, you will need to remove the unimportant things
that waste your time.

How do you ensure that you gain the maximum productivity out of each 24 hours of your life?

How do you ensure that as an entrepreneur lawyer you create work-life balance and a business that serves your life?

It can be done by taking the following steps:

How to Gain Clarity of Purpose

Step one – for creating work-life balance:

Gain clarity

It is essential that you set crystal clear vision, goals or however you decide to name it about what you want to achieve and why you want to achieve it. I have already dealt with the creation of a vision for your business in chapter one. I am not going to expand on it in here. This chapter is about your individual vision and your personal motive for wanting to achieve it?

Motivational gurus and most successful people say you need to love or be passionate about what you do. If you do not love what you do you will not enjoy doing it. While I do not disagree with them, what I find difficult with this concept is I have not heard a precise definition of passion.

What is passion? Because I have not heard an answer to this question, I prefer to stay away from the word passion. Instead I will use the word: reason. The reason is your internal 'why' for wanting to achieve your vision. I believe that it is our 'why' that lights up our fire and keeps us keeping on. The way I see it, the mission is more important than the means to achieving it.

My vision is five words: my son and my country.

Everything I do, I do to set an example to my son. So that when he grows up he will not have an excuse not to succeed. He will say to himself, my father came to this country, with little command of the language. He still managed to build a multi-million pound business. So what is my excuse?

Then I do for my country. Being an African I am of the belief that Africa will not develop until we Africans in the Diaspora return to help our individual countries with the expertise we have gained from the developed West. Even though I use my business as a vehicle for achieving my goals, my goals are crystal clear to me. I have never had a down day for the last few years because each day I remind myself of my 'why'; the reason.

My question to you is this; do you have your personal reason crystal clear? Do you know why you work twelve or fifteen hours per day? If you don't, you need to begin to search for it now because more than anything, the mission is what pulls you through the difficult times.

In Viktor Frankl's 'Man's Search for Meaning' he said; *"the meaning of life is found in every moment of living; life never ceases to have meaning, even in suffering and death…a prisoner's psycho-logical reactions are not solely the result of the conditions of his life, but also from the freedom of choice he always has, even in severe suffering. The inner hold a prisoner has on his spiritual self relies on having a faith in the future; once a prisoner loses that faith, he is doomed".*

How to Exploit Your Strength

Step two – for creating work-life balance:

Exploit Your Strength

As I researched the concept of work-life balance for this book, I came across two conflicting schools of thought on the subject of strength. One school of thought suggests that you need to focus on developing your strength and make your weakness irrelevant. The other trend of thought suggests that it is logical to work on both.

These information came from very credible sources two of which are; Brad Smart in his book "Top Grading" and Marcus Buckingham in his book "Now discover your strength". My dilemma was which one do I think is right to recommend my readers?

To answer this question, I am going to use my own situation as a case study.

I come from a non-English speaking country. Most Africans claim they originate from either a French or an English speaking country. When we arrive in England the mother of English, and try to communicate with English people, they seldom understand a single word of what we say. It is when faced with such situation that we come to the realisation that English is not our mother tongue. We speak something that sounds like English but it is not actual English.

I struggled with that scenario when I arrived in the UK. Like most foreigners I came to the realisation that I needed to relearn English. I tried working hard to improve my English. Furthermore, I also needed to work on my accent because with an African accent finding a decent job was proving to be a struggle. I tried and raised my spoken English to a point now that I am understood when I speak. However, my African accent remains. My dilemma now was; should I spend time trying to change my accent which may take a few years or do I exploit my ability to write well to my advantage?

To answer this question, I will refer to a few successful people. The last few years Tiger Woods has been struggling with his game of golf. However, it would take a brave person to argue that prior to his marital troubles he was not one of the best golfers ever to grace the planet earth. Here is a Tiger's secret, even at the top of his game in 2003; he was ranked number 123 in the world in sand trap. Would he have benefited from trying to improve his sand trap? Well Tiger thought otherwise, he instead decided to focus on enhancing his strength and making his weakness irrelevant. So that despite his handicap in sand saves he was still the best golfer in the world.

Pablo Picasso, Tom Cruise, Richard Branson, Leonardo Da Vinci, Thomas Edison, Jay Leno and Whoopi Goldberg top the list of very successful people who are dyslexic. Despite their disability, they did not focus on their weakness; instead they developed their strength to the point that their weaknesses became irrelevant.

In order to be able to achieve work-life balance, you need to discover your strength. When you do, harness it with power. Then work mostly on those things that relate to your strength and either delegate or eliminate those things that expose your weakness.

I outlined the process of discovering your strength in chapter three. So I will not be recapping it in this chapter. However, I urge you to return to chapter three, reread the information about discovering your strength. Then develop your work plan and schedule it in relation to your strength.

> This is Peter Drukker's take on the augment *"The effective executive knows that to get strength, one has to put up with weaknesses"*.

How To Structure Your Work Load For Maximum Productivity

Step three – for creating work-life balance:

Structure Your Work for Incremental Results

The best way to achieve work-life balance is to structure your work in such a way that you produce incremental results each step of the way. Most of us professionals feed on chaos; our work pattern is completely unstructured. That makes it difficult to achieve workflow. The most effective productivity strategy is to focus on your personal workflow pattern. Ask yourself; How can I structure my workload in such a way that it produces the desired results while at the same time providing me the freedom to engage in recreational activities?

To answer this question, I will return to Peter Drukker's statement in 'The Effective Executive'; he suggests that effectiveness results from the following:

- Record what you do with your time on a daily basis
- Ask yourself what is your contribution to your organisation
- Identify your strength and use that to increase your productivity
- Put first things first
- Make effective decisions that are not based upon sentiment

Here you have it.

In order to get a handle on your time, you need to:

- List the things you do during your work day
- Arrange them in order of priority in relation to your goals
- Focus on doing the most important things first
- Eliminate the things that are not absolutely necessary to achieving your goals
- Delegate low value tasks
- Stop engaging in activities that waste the time of your employees
- Institute good systems for information dissemination within your organisation

How to structure your workload

The ability to structure your work in a more productive manner is very essential for creating work-life balance. One of the reasons why lawyers overwork is that they lack the ability to complete tasks. Because you engage in time wasting activities in the name of multi-tasking and not focus on a single task you are unable to gain a sense of achievement at the end of your working day.

Consequently, you work harder and harder to get a sense of accomplishment. However, the harder you work the more difficult it is to accomplish any meaningful result because in the final analysis it is not about the amount of effort but the right effort. To effectively structure your workload, you need to adopt the following steps:

Step one – for structuring your workload:

Ask the right questions

The key to accomplishing tasks that produce results is firstly to identify the objective of the task. Whatever the task you embark on the first group of questions that you need to ask are:

- a) What is the goal of this task?
- b) What contribution would it make to the overall goal of the business?
- c) How would completing this particular task move me toward my end goal?

The next group of questions are:

- a) What is the beginning and end of the task?
- b) What would need to happen for me to know that I have completed this particular task?

The third question:

- What level of priority is this task to the overall scheme of what I am trying to accomplish?

The reason for these questions is to establish whether completing that particular task is a good use of your time at that very moment.

Step two – for structuring your workload:

Chunk it down

Assuming you have already gained clarity, which means that you already know where you are headed as a business and you have already listed your objectives in order of priority.

The next step is to chunk the individual task down into manageable chunks that can be completed on a daily basis.

Before starting each day, preferably the previous evening, list down the tasks that need to be accomplished.

Break them down into blocks of two hours; making provision for half an hour breaks between breaks.

Basically if you start work at 09:00, you ensure that the first two hours of your working day is used for the highest leverage activity. Let's say on that day you needed to complete an important report, you should ensure that the report writing is at the top of your agenda for the day. When you arrive at your office, you inform your assistant that except there is a nuclear explosion close to your office you are not to be disturbed.

You enter your office, switch off all distractions. You do not check your e-mails under any circumstances. Turn on your computer and get ready to start writing. While the computer is booting; do not engage in any activity that is not related to the report. While waiting for the computer to start, gather all the information you might need in relation to the report.

When your computer is ready, you dive into the report and force yourself to stay at it until the two hours elapse. After the two hours take half an hour break and start again. During the break you are not to engage in any work related activities just relax. If you follow this workflow structure on a daily basis, you will be more productive than you have ever been.

As entrepreneurs there may be other important things that you need to attend to during your work day. Those things need to also be scheduled into blocks of hours to ensure that they are completed at a set time. Probably after your first two blocks of two hours; you can take an hour or two to attend to other things and then return to your important tasks.

There are two things that need to be taken into consideration. The idea of this process is not to restrict your activities to this particular structure. We all have different dynamics, so one size does not fit all. What is true for all work is that to get it done effectively, it needs to be completed in blocks and that the most important and difficult tasks need to be completed first or else they will never be done. In Brian Tracy's 'Eat that frog', he suggests that if you completed your most important task at the start of your work day (the frog) the rest of the day would run smoothly.

Multi-tasking is never an effective way of working. To multi-task is to tell yourself *"I really do not want to get anything done"*.

Step three – for structuring your workload:

Create a Conducive Work Environment

One very important aspect of structuring workload is ensuring that your work environment is conducive for the type of work you are doing. You need to create a work environment that enables you to perform at your best. Few of the things that are necessary for the creation of a conducive work environment are:

- a) The right furniture
- b) The right electronic devices
- c) The right staff
- d) The right work equipment

How to Maintain High Energy Level Seven Days A Week

Step four – for structuring your workload:

Preserve Energy

Preserving energy is one of the most important things required to achieve work-life balance. So what role does energy play in work-life balance achievement?

Everything!

Without energy; it does not matter how grand or lofty your vision is, you have no chance of achieving it.

How can you acquire the energy required to achieve your vision?

Exercise

Exercise is another counterintuitive element of the work-life balance process. There is a conventional belief that we get tired after exercise. I am not a medical or fitness expert therefore I am not giving any medical advice but here is what I can say from my personal experience. Exercise completely jump starts my engine for the day; every day. I have what I call my morning rituals; one of those is exercising.

Whenever I go to the gym in the morning, the first few hours of my day are incredibly productive. I am pumped up. My creative juice is flowing and I am able to accomplish a lot within those first few hours. Now that I am writing a lot, in the evenings when I feel jaded and I still want to go on writing; I go for a swim. By the time I return home, I am fresh again; ready to ply on for another four to five hours.

Most professionals view exercise as a waste of time. They want to start their work day as early as possible. So going for a run or doing some form of exercise would delay their arrival at work. They end up working hard throughout the day without actually producing any results. Remember it is not the amount of hours you put in but what you put into those hours that matters. If you are half asleep or low on energy, no amount of caffeine will make you as productive as taking half an hour exercise in the morning.

If you read information about the lives of the most successful people in our world today without exception the first thing they do in the morning is exercise.

Food

I originated from Liberia, where rice is the staple; therefore, I am used to eating rice. In Liberia some people eat rice three times a day. I was not aware that eating white rice constantly demobilises me, until I learnt that certain types of food saps away one's energy. When I was taught that most white food saps away energy, I began to observe my state after eating white rice and behold every time I ate white rice after a few minutes, I felt like sleeping. When I am working and I eat rice, within half an hour I begin to feel sleepy.

Like white foods, there are so many foods that saps away your energy. As professionals you need to know those foods and stay away from them. Do not ever be caught with an excuse that because you are so busy, you do not have the time to eat right.

Did you know eating the wrong food affects your productivity? It does by forcing you to work longer hours in the hope that you will get the job done. I am not a dietician; therefore will not be giving you any dietary advice. What I will leave with you is this; certain foods make you more productive than others. So finding those foods that make you productive and cutting out food that saps your energy will more than quadruple your productivity.

Renewal

It goes without saying that rest is an important restorative. To me, rest means two things; adequate sleep and recreation. I am not going to tell you what you already know that you need to sleep at least eight hours a day. What you might not have given any serious thought to is the area of recreation. Like exercise, no one can be productive without recreation. We need to renew and rejuvenate our body on a daily basis. That is a requirement for productivity. A ten to fifteen minute walk a day can make a tremendous difference to your level of productivity.

Many of us started business because our bosses were horrible, but as time went on we have become to ourselves and our employees those bosses we once hated. Not resting in the day because you are so busy, is robbing yourself of the chance to relax. There is no way of explaining the feeling of walking in a park on a spring afternoon; no number of words can describe the emotional benefit that is derived from that and subsequently the increased productivity it brings to your day.

In order to be able to put a lot into the hours, you need to take steps to keep your energy level high. Exercising, eating well and resting are the best natural practices for maintaining high energy levels. Caffeine wouldn't cut it. Caffeine will keep you alert, but it would not make you productive.

> To be productive as an entrepreneur lawyer requires energy. You can only acquire energy through exercise, good food and rest.

How To Delegate For Productivity

Step five – for structuring your workload:

Recruit Great People

We dealt with the importance of having great people in an organisation (See chapters one and four). But as an entrepreneur; the reason you need to hire good people is that it frees you up to engage in other activities without worrying about the state of your business.

Many entrepreneur lawyers never switch off completely; even when you leave work. Entrepreneur lawyers tend to micromanage. You micromanage not because it is a bad habit that you picked up from childhood; you micromanage because you do not employ the right people in the first instance.

There are two reasons for this:

- As a lawyer you do not readily trust other people's judgement.
- You convince yourself that it does not make financial sense to hire an expensive employee at the start-up stage of your business.

With regard to the first issue, you need to realise that you were trained as a lawyer, not an entrepreneur. To run a successful law firm and achieve a 7 Figure income per annum, you will need help. Having your neighbour's wife or child moonlight as an assistant is good for a short period. However, to move from start-up to 7 Figure, you need well-trained and well-qualified people.

The reality is you cannot achieve 7 Figure as a lawyer all by yourself. It would never happen. Also, achieving 7 Figure in a legal firm requires that you have a well-qualified and experienced manager and quality support staff. I am not suggesting that you hire over-priced staff. Remember? 'A talent' do not come cheap but they are not an expense. They are an investment. Within a few months they will be able to pay for themselves and even generate profit. However, most importantly, they will give you the chance to engage in other activities that you require to provide you with the energy you need to grow your legal firm.

Creating System for Productivity

Step six – for structuring your workload:

Create Good Systems

We have already dealt with systems in chapter one. But it is essential to note that if you ever hope to achieve work-life balance through delegation, you will need to have good systems in place.

With a well-structured system, there will be no need to micromanage. A proper system will be clear on responsibility. It will also make it easier to monitor staff activities in your absence. Firstly because you spell out all procedures in writing; you make it easy for staff to follow them in your absence. This means they should not need to call you. Secondly, when you return to work, you can review the system for compliance and assign accountability.

A well organised system for your law firm, aids in the creation of a good work-life balance for you.

The achievement of work-life balance is as essential for productivity as it is for the growth of a 7 Figure business. However, in order for an entrepreneur lawyer to achieve a good work-life balance, you will first need to follow the above steps.

> As an entrepreneur lawyer, you require clarity about your mission. After clarity comes, "A talent" and good systems. Remember it is not about time management it is about self-management.

How to Create Work-life Balance

Action steps

I once listened to Tony Schwartz speak. He said he and another gentleman did research on the best tennis players in the world. They paid particular attention to the top two players. What they discovered was that all the top players had similar abilities and skills. What made the difference between the top two and the rest was what they did during play.

What the top two players did was in between play, they moved their racket from one hand to the next and at the end of each play they do not keep their eyes on the net. They kept their gaze somewhere other than the net and that gave them time to recover between plays.

The point he tried to make was that productivity and effectiveness do not require doing a whole lot of different things; it requires just doing some little things differently from others.

For example; just by changing the hands in which they held their rackets and allowing the playing hands to rest, the world's top two tennis players gained enormous advantage over their competitors.

> Achieving work-life balance does not require you to radically change the things you do; all it requires is for you to make some minute adjustments to the way you currently work.

I am in the business of information products creation. As a result of that, I spend long hours in front of my computer, either researching or writing. This places a lot of strain on my back, arms and shoulders. I had to go for a massage every week. What I did not know was that the reason I was in constant pain had nothing to do with the long hours I spent in front of the computer. It was the way my work station was set up.

I had a visit from an ergonomic expert who saw the way my work station was set up; advised me to make some changes and since that time I have had no more pain.

The point of this story is that in order for you to determine what would result in an effective work-life balance for you; you need to examine the way you currently do things. There are a few changes that you can make right now that would increase your level of productivity tenfold.

Do not dwell on the notion that entrepreneurship demands long painful hours of hard work. You can be successful as an entrepreneur just by doing a few things right.

Remember it is not the amount of hours you put into your work that is important, it is what you put into the hours that is more important. You can work for ten hours and produce a result that you could have produced with two hours of work if you operated at your optimal.

Achieving work-life balance requires that you take the following steps:

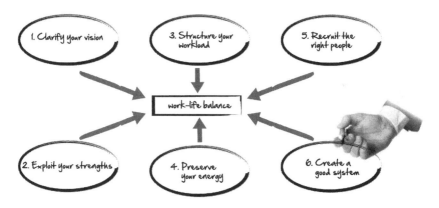

The biggest take away from this chapter has to be the application of the 80/20 or 95/5 rule. 95% of the things you are currently doing are only responsible for five per cent of the results you are producing. If it was the other way around, you will be able to increase your productivity tremendously. Analyse your current work day. You will find where the 95% is going to waste.

Transformation

You could be reading this book after attending several time management training courses. Furthermore, this might not be your first book on work-life balance. My question is; what changed after you attended time management seminars or read other books on work-life balance?

Have you attended motivational seminars? Did they change you?

> The fact of the matter is no one else can change you; it is only you who can change yourself. It does not matter how many time management or work-life balance seminars you attend or books you read; if you do not make the decision to change yourself, you will not change.

Harvard Psychologist and motivational guru David McClelland once said that change doesn't occur for one of four reasons:

- The system does not allow change
- There is no motivation to change
- We don't know what to do or how to do it
- We aren't able to do it

Do you know the reason that is preventing you from making the necessary change that would enable you to achieve work-life balance?

In dealing with systems in chapter one, I outlined the four stages of a business and the role of the entrepreneur in each of those stages. I also explained that one of the things that prevents most businesses from growing is the inability of the entrepreneur to evolve as the business move through the various stages.

As a professional entrepreneur, you must realise that a business is a moving target. It is either growing or declining. And each stage of your business reflects your level of development. If your business is growing into a 7 Figure business, it means you have evolved into a 7 Figure person. If your business is declining, it means you are moribund.

Albert Einstein once said; *"We cannot solve a problem with the same level of thinking that created that problem."* If you want to change and create work-life balance, you first need to change your level of thinking.

The reality is this; you cannot move your law firm from start-up to 7 Figure with the same level of thinking that you had when you started your firm.

You will need to transform yourself and evolve from the business start-up entrepreneur lawyer to a 7 Figure entrepreneur. You cannot build a 7 Figure law firm by working yourself to the ground. You need transformation.

In Charles Dickens' 1843 novel, 'A Christmas Carol' he told the story of Ebenezer Scrooge a ruthless businessman with no regard for anyone but himself. He treated his only surviving relative, friends and employees with the utmost contempt. Resented the poor and was never a happy man. He intended to spend Christmas on his own when he was visited by the ghost of his dead business partner who urged him to change his ways to avoid meeting the same fate as him.

The ghost walked him through his past, present and future, showing him how he was going to end up if he did not change his ways. This dream resulted in the transformation of Ebenezer Scrooge.

I do not have the power to walk you through your past, present and future, but what I know is this; an entrepreneur lawyer who cannot achieve work-life balance and cannot mutate with his business does not have a rosy future ahead of him.

Eben Pagan one of my favourite internet marketers and business trainers created a concept called 'Inevitability thinking'. The concept he said is setting up conditions that would force you to make a change.

You can apply this principle if you intend on achieving work-life balance. Build in mechanisms for accountability and consequences that would force you to take action. You need to ensure that the consequences are so painful that you are forced to act.

For example if you want to go on a holiday; book the holiday in advance. This will force you to make the necessary arrangements to ensure that your firm can run in your absence.

If you want to do exercise and you find it difficult exercising on your own, hire a personal trainer that would force you to follow through on your exercise regime. This is what 'Inevitability thinking' is about, setting up conditions that forces you to take action.

You will not be able to move your law firm from start-up to 7 Figure if you cannot muster the courage to discipline yourself to take the necessary actions.

You need to:

- Clarify your vision
- Exploit your strength
- Structure your workload
- Preserve your energy
- Recruit the right people
- Create a good system

Above all you need *'flow'*.

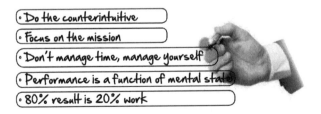

- Do the counterintuitive
- Focus on the mission
- Don't manage time, manage yourself
- Performance is a function of mental state
- 80% result is 20% work

Chapter Six: How to Create Productivity Metrics for your Legal Practice

Neuro Linguistic Programming (NLP) is a system that aids behavioural modification and change. The programme is based on four basic principles.

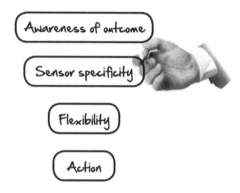

In the NLP programming framework, in order to achieve anything, one needs to articulate an outcome. This calls for the individual to say what he expects at the end of the process.

The next step is for the individual to clearly articulate an evident procedure for measurement of their outcome. In other words there needs to be a benchmark with which the outcome can be measured. The more feedback they gather, the more aware they are of the distance between where they are and where they are headed. In order to constantly improve, one has to be aware of the past and present position and future destination.

Sensor specificity is followed by flexibility. As the individual moves towards his outcome he receives constant feedback. Here he needs to have the flexibility to make changes along the way in line with that feedback. The best plans can never be considered ultimate until they are put to the test. Therefore, as the individual tests the plan, if he notices that certain aspects of the plan are impracticable, he needs to have the flexibility to make the necessary changes.

The final step requires one to take massive action. Extensive planning without action is a waste of time.

These are the fundamentals that form the base of NLP technology. In a way, these four pillars are critical for the achievement of any goal. The first half of this book has been based on the four plus one fundamental principles of a successful business:

As you apply the four plus one fundamentals to your business, there has to be a way in which you will be able to measure your progress. In most instances, the concept of achievement; good or great is subjective. What might constitute good or great to one person might not be that good to another person. Consequently, it is imperative that you have a universal benchmark for measuring achievement.

Why You Need a Business Metric

As a business, you need to be able to conduct a gap analysis between actual and potential performance. Gap analysis answers two simple questions.

- Where are we at this moment?
- Where is our final destination?

In the first chapters, I focused on the definition of your vision, good people, systems and marketing systems. Now that you have an understanding of what constitutes good people; good systems and a good marketing system, you can use it as a benchmark to picture where you are as a business and your final destination. With knowledge of your current position and final destination, you have the capability of conducting a gap analysis and measuring your level of progress along the way.

Be aware that most measurements are subjective because they are usually based on our experiences and programming. That is why it is imperative that you device independent tools to measure your progress. Independent tools are very essential when dealing with employees and partners.

If you were to pull your marketing manager over at the end of the quarter and complain that sales were not improving, you would need a set of facts that you can use to demonstrate the point. The saying in advertising is; 50% of advertising is wasted, the only problem is no one seems to know which 50% is wasted. As you learnt in chapter two on marketing, even advertising can be measured. However, in order to be able to measure the result of your advertising campaign, you need a set of metrics with which you can demonstrate that your campaign has either been a success or failure.

In every organisation five per cent of the staff produce 95% of the profit. The problem with most organisations is that they do not know which five per cent produces the 95%. Five per cent of any system is more efficient than the rest.

Could you imagine what would happen to productivity and the profit margin of your legal practice if you knew which five per cent of your staff produced 95% of your results? I will tell you. Your productivity will quadruple and your profit would go through the roof.

What if you were able to identify the five per cent of your sales people that were responsible for 95% of your sales? Your sales will skyrocket.

How to Identify Your Most Productive Five Per Cent

So how can you identify the five per cent of your system that is more efficient than the other 95%?

Here is how. Measure the input and output of each individual and department. The best way of knowing whether you are moving towards your goal as a business is to put in place the mechanism for measuring your progress each and every step of the way. The introduction of evident procedure that indicates whether you are moving towards; away from your goal or at a standstill is crucial for success.

When I consult with businesses, the overwhelming reason they give for lack of growth, is the lack of resources. However, as I dig into the organisation's resources, in nine out of 10 cases, it turns out that their lack of growth has little to do with a shortage of resources. Rather it is due to an uneven distribution of resources. That is; some areas that require more resources are starved while areas that require less are over resourced. What you need is the ability to strike the right balance and you can do that by measuring all activities in your legal practice with the right metrics.

The more successful businesses in the world are those with the ability to measure every aspect of their operations. It is therefore not surprising that hi-tech companies are among them. Their success results from their ability to test and measure every aspect of their operations. The ability to test and measure their activities gives them huge advantage. Furthermore, before producing a product they are capable of estimating to the closest penny how much they are going to sell.

The ability to measure is essential for the success of any endeavour. It is said that 98% of small businesses have no mechanism for measuring their business activities. The lack of measuring tools is also said to be responsible for the failure of most small businesses.

> In his book *"Business at the speed of thought"* Bill Gates writes; *"I have the simple but strong belief...How you gather, manage, and use information will determine whether you win or lose."*

> *"It would be nice, if all of the data which sociologists require could be enumerated,"* William Bruce Cameron said. *"Because then we could run them through IBM machines and draw charts as the economists do. However, not everything that can be counted counts, and not everything that counts can be counted".*

As a business, in order to develop the right mechanism for measurement; you need to know what components of your activities are measurable.

What You Should Measure

These are the three core principles that underpin any business measurement metric:

1. Everything can be measured
2. Most measurements are subjective
3. If it cannot be measured, it has not been done right

The following are the activities you need to measure in your legal practice:

- a) Marketing activities and results
- b) Customer acquisition and retention
- c) Financial performance
- d) Employee performance
- e) Business development
- f) Supplier performance
- g) Training and development

There are other elements of measurement that might be more appropriate for a legal practice. But the above metrics are applicable to most. Although you might be tempted to create lots of metrics; it is important that your metrics are limited to the core measurements of your business activities.

Every metric must be:

- Connected to the overall goals of your law firm
- Acceptable to all stakeholders
- Clearly measurable
- Directly linked to past, present and future performance of your legal practice

How to Develop Management Metrics for a Legal Practice

The process of developing management metrics for a legal practice starts with the development of a core metric. This could be a single marketing denominator such as the number of customer acquisitions per month, amount of profit per customer acquisition, profit per employee, or profit per transaction. There need to be a single organisation wide metric that is used as the core measurement for performance measurement of the organisation as a whole.

In his book 'Good to Great' Jim Collins explains the importance of core metrics in his three circles. He used Walgreens as an example.

Walgreens switched its focus from profit per store to profit per customer visit. Convenient locations are expensive, but by increasing profit per customer visit, Walgreens was able to increase convenience (nine stores in a mile) and simultaneously increased profitability across its entire system".

Every other metric is to be subordinated to the core metric and the core metric needs to be communicated throughout the organisation.

The next step in the process is to segment the metrics into the following categories:

A. Business visionary metrics: this relates to the vision you have for your legal practice. This metric answers the following questions:

1. Is your business progressing the way you envisaged from the start?
2. Are you achieving the goals you set for your business?

B. Management metrics: this relates to the actual running of the business and answers the question:

- How is the business performing in terms of cash flow, profit, operations and processes?

C. Systemic metrics: this relates to your systems and answers the questions:

1. Do you have the right systems in place?
2. Are your activities automated?
3. Can they be duplicated and replicated?
4. Are they transferable and teachable?

Let's now breakdown each metric to its individual components:

Marketing Metrics to Measure

For marketing metric the following needs to be measured:

- Quality and cost per lead
- Closing ratio
- Cost per customer acquisition
- Average sales
- Closing rate
- Number of appointments
- Number of closes per appointment
- Number of telephone calls per appointment
- Number of marketing messages sent before closing a sale: emails, leaflet etc.
- Number of calls in response to advert
- Number of customers gained as a direct result of advert

Employee Metrics to Measure

For employee performance metrics measure:

- Employee acquisition cost
- Employee training cost
- Employee turnover ratio
- Employee salary as a percentage of income
- Employee cost as a percentage of profit
- Employee production as a percentage of profit
- Employee production as percentage of cost of production
- Employee effectiveness
- Employee competency gap

Customer Relations Metrics to Measure

For customer relationship metrics measure:

- Number of customer acquisitions
- Cost per acquisition
- Percentage of retention
- Cost of retention
- Number of lost customers
- Customer complaints
- Customer satisfactions
- Customer value
- Profit per customer
- Value per transaction
- Repeat customer transactions
- Customer referral and recommendation

Financial Metrics to Measure

For financial metrics measure:

- Profit per transaction
- Cash flow situation
- Profit per customer visit
- Gross and net profit
- Return on investment
- Current and future income
- Current and future profit

Supplier Metrics to Measure

For supplier metrics measure:

- Achievement of objectives
- Quality of delivery
- Delivery time frame
- Cost of late delivery
- Profit per supplier
- Cost per supplier

Training Metrics to Measure

For supplier metrics measure:

- Financial result
- Behaviour change
- Level of knowledge acquired

Periodic Reviews

Every metric needs to be time bound. Therefore as you develop your metric, it is important that you attach a time frame for periodic review. The review period needs to be divided into quarterly, annual, five and ten years. It will need to be constantly monitored, assessed and improved.

Just a word of caution, no metric is written in stone; your metrics have to change to reflect growth and the changing business environment.

Assigning Accountability for Monitoring Metrics

Accountability for metric measurement and compliance is vital for business development.

Every section of the organisation ought to be assigned a different set of metrics, to monitor.

Below is a template of the level of accountability metric monitoring powers and the roles to which they are to be assigned.

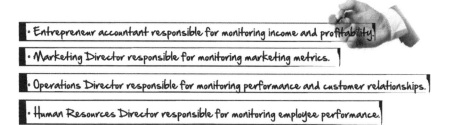

- Entrepreneur accountant responsible for monitoring income and profitability.
- Marketing Director responsible for monitoring marketing metrics.
- Operations Director responsible for monitoring performance and customer relationships.
- Human Resources Director responsible for monitoring employee performance.

Accountability also helps to reduce unnecessary conflict in the work place. When all employees understand the metric by which their work is going to be judged, it enables the smooth running of work assessments and appraisals.

Steps for developing your productivity metrics:

Step one

Develop a core metric

Step two

Segment your metrics into –

- Business visionary metrics
- Management metrics
- Systemic metrics

Step three

Conduct periodic review

Step four

Assign accountability

Chapter Seven: How to Identify The Obstacles to Your Business Growth

In chapter four on Work-life Balance, I relayed the story that Tony Schwartz the author of *"The Power of Full Engagement"* told about the world's top tennis players. A few key differences they had over their fellow players was that in between plays, they move their racket from the play hand and they do not keep their eyes on the net.

This information might sound trivial to anyone reading this book, but the reality is when it comes to success, it is the little things that make the difference. Tiger Woods was once the world's best golfer. As I write this book, he is now world number 25. What changed in Tiger's game that moved him from the world's best golfer to 25th in the world? He had a few injuries but his main problem is mental. From the moment his marital problems surfaced, he lost the killer instinct that once made him the world's best golfer.

If you are a football lover and you are familiar with English football you will know that the FA Cup features all divisions in England and Wales. And on many occasions the teams that make it to the FA Cup final are the second division or bottom of the table teams. This is not because the big teams don't want to win the FA Cup but the lesser teams out play them. Granted in the qualification stages, the bigger teams field mostly second team players. But as lesser teams manage to defeat the second team players of bigger teams they gain confidence and by the time they encounter the first team players of bigger teams in the later stages of the competition, they are no longer intimidated by them. This is the reason why lighter teams make it big in the FA Cup.

The point I want to make is; despite the fact that the bigger teams have highly rated multi-million pound players the lesser teams are able to match them man for man and even defeat them. This is because there is only a slight difference between the top premiership players and those who play for the bottom of the table teams or the second division teams. But that tiny difference is enough to keep the top teams at the top of the table.

This hypothesis does not only apply to football. We see it in every sport; the top ten players all have similar abilities. The difference is just a few things that the top performers do which the rest do not do. The reason why these few things continue to keep the top athletes at the top of their game is, those athletes know those few things and athletes at the bottom half of the table don't know those things.

In his book *"The Tipping Point: How Little Things Can Make A Difference"* author Malcolm Gladwell defines a tipping point as *"the moment of critical mass, the threshold, the boiling point."* One of the ideas he introduced in his book was a concept called "The Stickiness Factor". "The Stickiness Factor" is the specific content of a message that renders its impact memorable. As an example he used the popular children's television programme Sesame Street. The introduction of a moppet increased children's attention span. Then there is the university campus tetanus vaccination leaflet in which the inclusion of a map in the leaflet inspired a threefold increase in student uptake of the vaccine. In chapter after chapter throughout the book, Gladwell refers to a series of little things that made a big difference to businesses and people.

The point I want to make with the above examples is this; if you are not making 7 Figure at present in your legal firm, or if your legal firm is not growing, the issue preventing it from happening might boil down to just a single simple obstacle. However, in order to remove that stumbling block that is preventing you from achieving your goal, you first need to identify it.

As children we were taught by our parents to 'never give up'. In school, at work or in society as whole, the concept of never giving up continues to be reinforced. When we open our own business, we are also preprogramed from the start that certain things have to be done in a certain way and that we should expect certain outcomes at a certain time. This programming has become our guide. Programming such as: you do not make profit until your third year of business or that you cannot employ extra staff until you have a certain amount of income.

This programming is responsible for the failure of many legal firms. When we run into difficulties, instead of dissecting the problem to discover the root cause, we just continue doing things the same way in the name of not quitting. The reality is this, if you are doing the wrong thing, it does not matter how hard or long you do it, it will never become right. If you are headed east towards sun set, it does not matter how hard or fast you run or how hard you try, you will not find sun set.

One of society's programming is practice makes perfect. So we observe talented people go to waste because they feel they have practiced hard without result. Why? Simply because they do not know that practice does not make perfect rather it is perfect practice that makes perfect.

The Best frameworks for Identifying the Bottleneck to Your Business

In order to effectively tackle any problem, the first step must be to identify the root cause of the problem. When your legal firm is not growing according to plan, instead of putting in more hours and trying harder doing the wrong thing, the most appropriate course of action should be to stop and ask the simple questions:

- Why is my legal firm not growing?
- What or where is the bottleneck?

It is only when you are able to identify the bottleneck and remove it would your legal firm get on a growth trajectory. For example, if your sales team is under performing, instead of blaming them and thinking they are incompetent; you first need to investigate if they were the right people for the job in the first place. You should also check out your training regime.

Were they given the appropriate training for the job? Next, you need to check your recruitment department; did they recruit the wrong people?

When you address issues in this manner, you will readily identify the root cause; instead of focusing on the symptoms. The best tool ever developed for carrying out this process is Eli Goldratt *"Theory of constraint (TOC)"*.

Used efficiently TOC serves two purposes. It helps in creating a framework for achieving your goals and it also serves as a diagnostic tool for identifying your core constraint.

Even though TOC is the best problem solving framework ever created, it is not as widely used as it should be. The reason for this is that it is very complicated and the majority of people resent complicated models.

I have listened to Mr Goldratt the creator of TOC speak. He said that as a physicist, he does not like complications, because the belief in physics is that even a kid can complicate things.

As I listened to him, he sounded to me like an artist who has created what he considers a magnificent work of art but no one seems to understand what it is. That's the situation with Mr. Goldratt and TOC. For him it is so simple, everyone should be able to practice it without difficulty but for someone like me trying to teach it to the lay man, it can be very daunting.

I have struggled to teach TOC. I felt to myself it may be me who had not grasped the concept. However, one day I watched Rich Scheferen struggle to teach it too. Rich is one of the smartest business coaches in the world. So if Rich can struggle to teach TOC then what hope is there for someone like me.

As I pondered whether to include TOC in this book, I got an epiphany at the gym. It will not be a good idea to throw the baby out with the bath water. Simply because the framework is complicated does not mean it cannot be simplified. It is a great framework; all that was required is a bit of a modification to make it understandable and digestible to the ordinary mind.

What you have now is a revised version of TOC specifically designed to help legal firms diagnose the obstacles preventing them from achieving their goal of making a 7 Figure income annually.

To move your legal firm from start-up to 7 Figure in twelve months using the TOC framework, you will need to go about the process as follows:

How to Identify the Bottleneck to Your Business Growth

The Goal

At the top of your diagram you place your goal which in this case is to make 7 Figure annually.

The Critical success factor (CSF)

The next step in the process is to identify your critical success factors (CSF). Your CSFs are those elements you must have in place in your legal firm that would enable you to achieve your goal.

In this case they are five:

1. Visionary leadership or clear vision
2. Great people
3. Good system
4. Good marketing system
5. Good business model

The current situation

Step three in the process is to state your current situation. You have a goal of achieving a 7 Figure income per annum. The critical success factors for doing so are:

- Visionary leadership or clear vision
- Great people
- Good system
- Good marketing system
- Good business model

The critical question that this part answers is: do you have those in place in your legal firm right at this very moment?

If not,

- What do you have in place at present?
- And the next question is: why don't you have them in place?
- What is preventing you from putting them in place?

This last question now takes you to the final step which is the core constraint.

The core constraint

There might be several factors that are preventing you from having your critical success factors in place. However, amongst those elements there is one; when you remove, the dominos will fall. It is like the lever. When you turn the lever, the rest of the structure will turn along with it. It is usually a single lever. To find it requires that you keep asking yourselves the question: 'Why?'

For example:

Why don't you currently have great people?

- Because the HR department is finding it difficult to attract great people.

Why is the HR department finding it difficult to attract great people?

- Because the HR manager has not received the requisite training for recruiting great people?

Why hasn't the HR manager received the requisite training for recruiting great people?

- Because there are no funds for training HR personnel.

Why are there no funds for training HR personnel?

As you continue to ask the question; 'why?' you will be able to identify the core problem. When it is addressed you will remove the obstacles preventing your legal firm from growing.

In my experience, in the majority of the cases the core constraint preventing a small business from achieving its goal is the entrepreneur lawyer himself. It mostly comes down to the skill set of the entrepreneur lawyer. Most of the time, it is either the entrepreneur lawyer is so much of a technician that he is unwilling to think and behave like an entrepreneur or he has not grown with the business, instead he still possesses the business start-up skills.

The following is a list of other constraints:

- Lack of clients
- Lack of high paying clients
- Lack of "A talent"
- Lack of good marketing infrastructure
- Lack of good marketing staff
- Lack of good administrative staff

TOC is a very effective problem solving tool when used efficiently. All that is required is total honesty on the part of those using the tool. They need to ensure that they understand that the essence of the process is not finger-pointing but problem identification and solving.

Chapter Eight: How to develop a legal succession plan

Author Jim Collins in *'Good to Great'* introduced to concept of *"Level five leadership"*. According to Mr. Collins, there are five levels of leadership:

> *"Level 1 relates to individual capability, Level 2 to team skills, Level 3 to managerial competence, and Level 4 to leadership as traditionally conceived. Level 5 leaders possess the skills of levels 1 to 4 but also have an "extra dimension": a paradoxical blend of personal humility and professional will. They are somewhat self-effacing individuals who deflect adulation, yet who have an almost stoic resolve to do absolutely whatever it takes to make the company great, channeling their ego needs away from themselves and into the larger goal of building a great company. It's not that Level 5 leaders have no ego or self-interest. Indeed, they are incredibly ambitious— but their ambition is first and foremost for the institution and its greatness, not for themselves... Level 5 leaders are comfortable with the idea that their companies will tick on without them, reaching even greater heights due to the foundations they laid down. The fact that most people will not know that the roots of that success trace back to them is not an overriding concern".*

One chronic malady affecting many law firms that is causing them to shut down at the end of the founder's tenure is the lack of succession planning. As Mr. Collins pointed out, part of the quality of "level five" leadership is the willingness and ability to set successor up for success.

Succession planning refers to the intended activities, processes and programs put in place by a law firm to guarantee a smooth transfer of responsibilities and leadership to a succeeding generation of lawyers and managers. Essential to the success and long term endurance of a law firm is a well mapped out succession plan that immediately takes effect and maintain the firm's competitive advantage in the marketplace.

In the majority of law firms, the entrepreneur lawyer maintains leadership of the firm until he is incapacitated and lack the ability to perform effectively without making any provision for succession after he exits the scene.

For many law firms, succession planning is a somewhat taboo subject for fear of upsetting senior partners. However, the reality is people do get old therefore have to retire. Furthermore, there may be other circumstances such as illness, accident or personal matters that may prevent senior partners from fulfilling their duties effectively. Consequently, it is incumbent upon legal firms leadership to make succession planning a priority. Succession planning needs to be considered from the very onset of the firm when the mission and vision statements are being prepared.

Other factors that succession planning must take into consideration are key legal personnel suddenly deciding to terminate employment, other law firms approaching key employees with employment opportunities leading to termination of employment, a decrease in value of the firm or even vital employees wanting to move into a different position within the firm requiring a different skill set.

In order for a law firm to be successful, it is imperative that the leadership possess broad range of experiences, business development skills and expertise within their field. Often, the senior partner or practice manager will be the motivating force behind the law firm and in the event of retirement or other emergency situation, there is no one of equal experience to fill their shoe.

The following are a few reasons why succession planning is absolutely imperative for a law firm:

Function

Succession planning facilitates the smooth transfer of power from one leader to the next in the events that it becomes necessary.

Identification

Senior executives, human resource, and even board members have adequate time to participate in identifying next generation leaders and talented managers who will take over departmental or key function.

Considerations

Next generation leaders are groomed and nurtured into their roles in preparation for their eventual take over.

Benefits

Successful transition of business leaders and managers can ensure proper business continuation, minimize disruption and keep employees motivated to pursue long-term corporate objectives and business goals.

Factors to be considered in legal firm succession planning:

Effects

It is essential to take into consideration how succession planning affects the long-term future of your firm.

Essentials

Succession plans map out potential candidates to replace existing people in positions for a number of years going forward.

Need

Every organization leaders and workers will not work indefinitely. At some point, all employees retire, leave or abandon their positions for other reasons.

Internal recruitment

Succession planning encourages generic promotion. This encourages organisation to recruit top talents that appreciate the opportunity of growing within your firm.

How to develop a legal succession plan?

In order for an entrepreneur lawyer to truly develop a successor he needs to bring on new employees capable of succeeding him when the need arises. The lack of planning can place stress on both the entrepreneur lawyers' staff and family as they struggle to cope with an unexpected event.

Steps for developing your legal firm succession plan:

Step one – Ensure client files contain sufficient detail so that in the event of an emergency, another lawyer taking over the files can immediately be brought up-to-date with the client's situation.

Step two – Obtain insurance containing disability policy to cover requirements in the event of loss of earning and also to cover the costs associated with hiring another lawyer to administer the firm and cover cash flow requirements until the firm gets back to normality.

Step three – Keep time and billing entries current to keep tract of the firm's obligations.

Step four – Pre-arrange a formal agreement with a colleague or another lawyer who can step-in immediately if you are not able to perform your duties.

Step five – Consider including provisions in retainer agreements as actions to take in the event of an emergency.

Step six – Ensure that you have a valid will including any terms required to deal with business-related issues.

Step seven – Consider whether a power of attorney is required to deal with trust legal issues or your firm generally.

Step eight – Ensure staff, partners, associates and family members are aware of your secession plans.

Steps for implementing successful succession planning:

Step one – Devise a succession plan policy that clearly outlines the ways in which your legal firm will address both anticipated and unexpected leadership changes. This policy should contain details of who will oversee managerial succession and the process for selecting a suitable successor.

Step two – Identify a candidate or two who will be trained to succeed senior management when the time comes. The successor should be introduced to your staff, clients and community early providing the boss-in-training authority to run the operation while still under your direction.

Step three – Maintain up-to-date office limitation and client file diary systems to accurately reflect all deadlines and all reminders so that next steps on files can be easily reviewed.

Step four – Utilize the performance review process to gain transparency of the accomplishments and shortcomings of individual employees as they relate to future leadership possibilities.

Step five – Maintain an office procedure manual outlining key practice aspects and a list of all essential contacts.

Having a good plan for choosing future leadership is fundamental to the long-term future of a law firm. Current partners and key employees cannot continue in their roles forever. A succession plan will make the transition smooth and less stressful. A succession plan will help explain who has the decision-making responsibility to appoint new leaders and involves grooming other employees to succeed managers when they leave the firm.

Create succession plan based upon your vision

Identify candidates with leadership qualities

Groom the individuals to succeed you

Chapter Nine: How to Effectively Handle Change in the Corporate Legal Business Environment

The decision to include this chapter in the book was made after I read 'Hope Is Not a Method – What Business Leaders Can Learn from America's Army' by Gordon R. Sullivan and Michael V. Harper. The idea of learning business lessons from the military might appear a bit strange for some people. For others learning lessons from the U.S. Army might even be a little uncomfortable.

For those in the first group who might not see the link between the military and the business world, I ask you to suspend your disbelief. Give me the benefit of doubt and just read this chapter. I promise you will not find a better lesson on change anywhere else. And for those who might be a little uncomfortable with lessons from the U.S. Army, I ask that you place your political views aside just for a few minutes and read this chapter. The benefit you will derive from it will outweigh political persuasions.

Business Lessons from the U.S. Army

In their book, the authors did a fine job of explaining how the U.S. Army transformed itself from a Cold War Army to an organisation equipped to confront the 21 century warfare. The U.S. Army has almost always been a reactive force. Understandably so, as a nation the U.S. has never really faced any credible threat from other nations and it is the biggest and most powerful nation on earth. This is not to underestimate the danger of terrorism which threatens the very existence of Western civilisation. But because terrorists are not a country, the role of the army is a bit diminished in the fight against terrorism.

The only credible threat would have come from Europe and Asia, however geographical location gives the U.S. a natural defence against attacks from Europe or Asia.

The fall of the Berlin Wall and the reduction in the threat posed by the Soviet Union, forced the U.S. to rethink its foreign policy priorities as well as its defence strategies. During the Cold War the U.S. Army primarily trained to take on the Russians who were the enemy. With the end of the Cold War the U.S. Army changed its strategies to cope with an ever transforming world.

How did they do that? How did they transform an organisation of 1.5 million people with bases in more than a hundred countries into an institution fit for purpose?

According to the authors, they accomplished this by adhering to the following principles:

- Understanding that change is difficult

- Beginning the process with shared values

- Mapping out the desired result upfront

- Changing the critical processes

- Engaging each and every member of the army

- Creating flexibility into the process

- Finding the balance between the present and the future

- Understanding that better, is becoming something different that will not only survive today but will be capable of sustaining tomorrow

- Constant application of the process and tweaking it as it moved along

As you can see, there is nothing military about the actions the army took towards change as evidenced by the ten steps outlined above. What the U.S. Army did to create an evolving army can be successfully applied to any business organisation.

How to Apply U.S. Army Business Lessons to Your Business

The way we do business has changed dramatically since "Industrial Revolution". At that time the desired result was speed. The introduction of mechanisation in production which gave man the ability to produce enough to meet the demands of a growing population changed the demand from speed to quality. The 1900s was about quality.

The 21st century has its own dynamics. The focus is no longer on speed or quality; it is now on 'total customer experience'. The emergence of the internet brought with it infinite consumer choice and revolutionised the way the world does business.

There was a time when landlords controlled the factors of production and distribution. The Industrial Revolution changed all that. It shifted the balance of power to the owners of the machines.

The internet age, has forced an end to a monopolisation of the factors of distribution. Now, no single individual or group of people controls information or the distribution channels. And the capacity of emerging markets to lower the cost of production means that the monopolisation of production by a few is no longer possible.

What this means is that just about anyone can create and market a product to anyone, no matter what part of the world they live. At present there is no big or small company. On the net, a small company in a dusty New Delhi ghetto can take on a multi-national conglomerate in London or New York.

This is because the focus is no longer about speed or quality but 'total customer experience' and value. The easy to access information brought about by the internet means that customers are more informed these days than they were five or ten years ago.

The following points are so significant I will endeavour to repeat them:

- The factors of distribution have changed
- Customers/clients are more informed than they were five or ten years ago

This means that corporate lawyers cannot use the same strategies they used five or ten years ago. Most professional firms that cease to exist have died because they failed to evolve with time. The 21st century is about two things:

- 'Total customer experience'
- Value

What is Total Customer Experience?

Today there are cries all over the UK and in many Western countries that the retail industry is under threat. The UK government, the Australian government and many other Western governments are fully involved in efforts to save their retail industries. The big issue with them is that they are not dealing with the core issues facing the industry; instead, they are dealing with the symptoms.

What is the problem facing the retail industry? It is plain and simply the industry is unable to change with the times. With the internet, consumers now have the luxury of ordering merchandise from the comfort of their home and their purchases can be delivered in twenty-four to forty-eight hours. Even grocery shopping is now growing online.

With the massive change brought about by the internet, how can brick and mortar retailers continue to entice customers to their shops?

This is the question the retail industry is failing to answer. Like the manufacturing and automobile industries, instead of finding answers to this question, they SOS their respective governments and hope to be rescued.

Rolls-Royce was once the pride of Britain. The finest automobile ever conceived by the human brain. Today it is owned by the Germans. The ruins of manufacturing towns all around the UK are testament to an entire industry that has taken its place in the business cemetery.

The brick and mortar retail sector is not that far from similar fate as ghost towns appear in city after city all over the UK. It is an industry that has failed to realise that this century is about 'total customer experience' and value.

I cannot remember the last time I entered a book or entertainment store. I do buy a lot of books; however, I do all my purchases on-line. When I want to watch a film I just download it. I download my music from iTunes. Now that I am able to get my books, music and videos from the internet, why would I want to go to a store? I could also do my groceries shopping online; I have many friends who do their groceries shopping online.

However, I do go to the supermarket almost every morning. Why? It wakes me up. From the gym I deliberately pass through the super-market just to smell the aroma of fresh bread coming through the store vents. For me it is equivalent to passing by a Starbucks café early in the morning with its smell of freshly brewed coffee.

This for me is 'total customer experience'. People go to retail stores for different experiences.

As you read through this chapter the question that needs to be going through your mind now is; what experience do customers have when they interact with your legal practice?

Here's the answer to the question: what could brick and mortar retailers can to lure the likes of me back to their store. They need to develop "Adaptive Capacity" – the ability to adapt to the changing retail environment.

Do you have enough "Adaptive Capacity" engrained in your legal practice?

What is Value?

I have already dealt with value in depth in chapters one and three, therefore I will not go into it in any detail in this chapter. However, for the sake of clarity of our current subject it would not hurt to just skim over it once more.

Value is a deal that brings measurable benefit to all of the parties involved in a transaction. A key phrase here is; measurable benefit. Value has to be sensory specific to eliminate the ambiguity and ensure that it results in benefit for both parties involved. It is imperative that the results or outcomes are agreed upon before the commencement of the transaction. I will now use an article I wrote in December 2011 to illustrate this point further…

Case Study

I attended the Nativity play with my three year old son in December 2011. At the end of the play not one parent in the hall had a dry eye. Even me, who consider myself a hard man from a war-torn country.

As I drove my son back home, it struck me that the nursery had managed to pull off something very spectacular. All the kids were between the ages of two and four years old and the nursery succeeded in making them perform a play. Except for a few glitches they all held their own with their lines.

However, as the emotion wore off, I began replaying the entire episode in my head through my marketing lenses. It hit home; "That was value". We do receive cards and little gifts from the nursery for occasions such as Christmas, Father's or

Mother's Day; even though those are always well appreciated, they are never hair raising.

Seeing my three year old perform was magical. How much would I have paid the nursery for that moment? One million pounds? Ten million? Why not try a billion pounds? It was priceless!

How much is a pill that prevents you from suffering a heart attack worth to you? That was what watching my son perform in that play worth to me.

Whenever the concept of value is discussed in a marketing setting, most of the time it is attributed to a gift. Old school sales and marketing lawyers advise trainees to send gift cards, anniversary cards or emails, fruit baskets or event tickets to their prospects. They are also advised to keep in touch through email newsletters or some other form of written or oral communication.

The reality is this, while gifts are good, they do not provide value. With the exception of fortune 500 companies where the person signing the pro-forma is not using his own money. The majority of entrepreneurs who spend their own money are busy people who would careless about fruit basket or newsletter.

It is a distraction that they can do without. Except of course if the information being sent would save them from a heart attack which is entrepreneurial code: for make profit.

I receive a minimum of 150 emails per day. I have to weave my way through those emails to extract the relevant from the irrelevant. Do you think I really care if someone sent me a Happy Thanks Giving or Merry Christmas email?

When I receive an email from a sales person that says 21 ways to produce products in 24 hours, that is the type of email that would grab my attention and make me want to open it. Furthermore, I will look forward to receiving more emails from that person. I bet you the majority of entrepreneurs think and feel the same way.

Before sending anything to a prospect or to your existing client, ask yourself these two questions:

1. Is it valuable enough to save him from a heart attack?
2. Would I want to receive such a message myself?

The nursery sending me cards and gifts hardly ever caught my attention. However, seeing them presenting my son in that beautiful moment was more valuable to me than all their cards and gifts put together.

Think about it, what can you give to your prospects or clients that would make tears stream down their cheeks? That is value!

How to Change Your Legal Firm

Value in relation to business is focused on profit. Any business to consumers' transaction is more about emotion. The question that might be running through your mind now is how do you quantify emotion? It's easy, just identify the outcome the individual is seeking upfront and as long as you provide them that outcome, you have provided value.

Change is a constant, with the fast pace of technological development, the next few decades will see change move at the speed of sound. The question you will need to ask yourself is this:

- Will you be a creator of change or a creature of change?
- Will you be a victim of change or will you rather be a master of change?

That is your pick but either way change will come.

The baby elephant in captivity is prevented from roaming about by a tiny rope tied to one of it legs and to a wooden post in the ground. The elephant is confined to an area determined by the length of the rope. The baby elephant tries to break the rope but it can't. After a few attempts it stops trying resigned to the fact that it cannot break the rope. When it grows up into a thousand pounds creature, it can easily break the rope but it never even tries, believing that it still can't.

The above information is a good metaphor to describe the state of mind of most entrepreneur lawyers. Like the thousand pounds elephant that does not know its powers, many entrepreneur lawyers do not know their strength.

There are two things about change currently affecting legal practices. Firstly like the elephant, many legal practices are stuck in the past. They still operate with the 19th century paradigm. And it is just wrong for this age and time.

Secondly, there are lawyers who still do not realise how easy it is to succeed as an entrepreneur lawyer in the 21st century business environment. With the removal of the monopoly over the factors of distribution, the balance of power is now in the hands of small and medium size legal practices. Attempting to change a fortune 500 company could be like trying to turn a massive ship around. Small and medium size legal practices on the other hand are like speed boats, you can turn them at will.

Remember this; on the computer screen, your small legal practice is as big as the biggest legal practice. You can outperform them and you can take them on and win. But you have to first change from the mentality of the baby elephant and realise that you can break the rope, turn around your speed boat and head towards the 21st century business environment. It is only then that you will be able to move your legal practice from perpetual start-up to a 7 Figure per annum business.

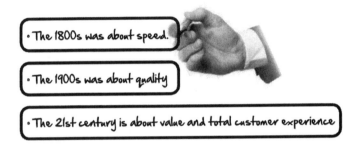

- The 1800s was about speed.
- The 1900s was about quality
- The 21st century is about value and total customer experience

Chapter Ten: How to Create an Legal Partnership that Works

To be a partner in a law firm is the aspiration of most young lawyers. Partnership means that they are no longer just salaried employees; but they get to be part of the decision making process and share in the firm's profit.

The road to a legal partnership is not paved with gold. In fact it can be a long and tedious process. However, when it is finally realized, especially if it is with a successful law firm, the payoff can be well worth the wait.

Law firms are known to call on prospective partners to invest or provide a bank loan guarantee, which could be an amount equal to the value of the shares of the existing partners.

Note this well. Before you decide on accepting a new partner into your law firm; you ought to scrutinize the strengths and weaknesses of the individual. Furthermore, never lose sight of the fact that a major reason for the failure of most law firms is the inability of lawyers to market their services.

Consequently, know the strengths and weaknesses of each individual who is being considered for partnership. It is very crucial for the success of the law firm. For example if two really good lawyers decide to form a partnership but neither of them know how to sell or run a business, despite their great legal minds, the law firm will fail or struggle to survive.

As I pointed out in chapter one, there are universal principles that apply to every type of business. They hold true whether the business is a law firm or a cold water business in the middle of the Sahara Desert. The principle of partnership is one of those principles. The principles of partnership state that for a partnership to be successful; everyone involved must have qualities that complement the others in the partnership.

If a law firm decides to bring in a partner; that person should not be drafted simply for his brilliant legal mind. The practice should make a point to think through his entrepreneurial ability; his marketing and his management ability. If he has a portfolio of big clients, that makes it easier. Then again, a really good lawyer could be offered top notch incentives to hold him in your firm; particularly if the move to make someone a partner is to avoid losing him.

Creating a partnership is never a technical decision. By this I mean an individual cannot be accepted as a partner because he is a good lawyer. Partnership is more like a business decision. And it has to stay that way if you desire your law firm to succeed. In addition to his professional contribution, every partner must make a business contribution.

When you have a successful legal business, you can attract and pay for the best legal minds in the country. However, if you have the best legal minds and you do not have business acumen, your law firm will fail. The legal business like all businesses is a competitive business. Therefore, business decisions have to be taken strategically.

Issues to consider in a partnership

Interpersonal problems

Ensure that the individual being considered for partnership is known to the other partners on a personal basis. In business there is always the possibility of interpersonal conflict developing when the business is under stress. The business of law is a very stressful business. It is different from preparing a legal brief when the only thing at stake is your client's interest. When it is people's own money and future on the line, the reaction can be completely different. This is why it is imperative that the partners know each other on a personal basis before making the decision to get into a partnership.

Personal stability

Apart from know-how, hard work and honesty; a potential partner needs to be emotionally stable. This is a very crucial point because getting into partnership with an individual who is unstable, is setting up your law firm for failure. Law firms fail because a partner decides to walk away from the partnership at a very pivotal point in the business, for personal reasons.

Integrity

Integrity is not always recognised as an aspect of business. But it is a very critical one. Business is based upon trust. Without trust, there can be no business transaction. Consequently, it is imperative that before inviting someone to become a partner in your law firm, that you either know the person personally or your background checks have cleared him.

If you do not bank on paying someone for the rest of his life to relax at a holiday resort in the Caribbean, conduct thorough background check before signing a partnership agreement. An employee you can dismiss, letting go of a partner is more complicated. You could prevent him from working in the law firm, but you will still have to continue to pay his dividend.

If a lawyer uses underhand tactics to win cases; it might bring glory to your firm. But it should also flag up your yellow alert. That's because it concerns the integrity of the person. Dishonest partners have run many businesses to the ground. So do not dismiss dishonesty as operational practice.

How to make legal partnership work

Here are steps for making your legal partnership work:

Step one – Create a vision statement for your practice. Be sure it expresses long term objectives. Vision statements should be inspiring; comprehensible, concrete and precise.

Step two – Identify specific roles and responsibilities of each partner and ensure that individual strengths, weaknesses, interests and talents are taken into consideration.

Step three – Outline the profit sharing arrangement. A simple 50-50 proposition may sound fair, but if one partner is solely responsible for generating profits, an extra commission that reflects this commitment might be suitable.

Step four – Determine the point of contact for clients and employees and decide whether individual roles will change from engagement to engagement. Clients should view your partnership as faultless and know precisely whom to contact.

Step five – Address how conflicts or split decisions will be resolved. Partnerships can be particularly susceptible to differences that are subjective in nature.

Step six – Determine how you will work as a team to generate new business; if for example the partners attend a networking or business event together or individually. The decision has to be made before hand and specific duties assigned before, during and after the event.

Step seven – Discuss problems honestly and openly. You probably formed the partnership because you share a good connection, mutual respect and commonalities. Solving problems or difficult issues should build confidence and strengthen a partnership.

Step eight – Celebrate your successes. Many businesses give people grieve over the deal they lost but they do not celebrate small victories that help build a successful partnership.

Partnerships could help you take advantage of great opportunities. Partners can naturally share resources and knowledge and achieve objectives. A good partnership business will break new grounds even if there seems to be difficulties along the way.

How to identify a good legal partner

Here is a list of steps for identifying the ideal partner for a law firm.

Step one – Find an individual who shares your values, entrepreneurial spirit and vision. This is the most important component for choosing a partner for your firm. There is going to be the need for constant communication, decision making and goal setting as you work together. Therefore, if your partner is someone who is a non-conformist, argumentative or unwilling to consider others point of view, there will be constant tension in the relationship.

Step two – Find an individual who brings diverse skills and experience to the relationship. A good business partnership should have skills that support and complement each other. No single person is good at everything. If you have great interpersonal skills but poor business finance skills; consider a partner who understands the business of law. The more skills you and your partner bring to the partnership the easier it will be to grow your firm.

Step three – Find a partner with less personal baggage. If your partner has serious challenges in his personal life, it may carry over into the business. It is nice to be willing to give someone a chance, but running a small business takes focus, time and a huge amount of energy. If your partner is dealing with one personal crisis after another you may find yourself carrying the weight of the business.

Step four – Find a partner who can offer resources and credibility to your law firm. It is great to have a law firm partner that has financial resources, but there are other contributions a partner can bring to your law firm, that are just as valuable. A partner with a strong business network, industry connections, client list, quality credentials and expertise can also increase the value of your law firm and improve your chances of achieving long term success.

Step five – Choose a partner who practices good personal and business ethics. Only enter into partnership with someone you can trust. Look for someone who values honesty, integrity and business ethics. A poorly chosen law firm partner may steal from your business, take your ideas or clients to start their own law firm or break laws that could get your law firm into trouble.

Step six – Respect is a key element of a successful partnership. You should never partner with someone who you do not respect. The main purpose of partnership formation is to achieve success as a team. You may not value the opinion and efforts of someone you do not respect at least on a professional level. You also want to partner with someone who will show you respect as a partner, business professional and as the founder of your business.

Partnership is a valuable tool for moving a law firm from start-up to 7 Figure. However, like every aspect of your business, it has to be managed well, to succeed.

Develop your firm's vision

Outline the role and responsibilities of each individual and position in the firm

Outline the calibre of candidate expected to fill those positions

Outline the profit sharing arrangement

Outline frameworks for conflict resolution

Summary

I being an entrepreneur myself understands that as entrepreneurs our time is finite. Therefore when we need answers to our questions, we need them as fast as possible.

This is the reason why I have summarised each chapter of the book in the section. So if you ever felt overwhelmed and you did not know where to start, just open this section and follow the steps for implementing the ideas in each of the chapters.

This is your checklist, I urge you to take advantage of it.

Chapter One Summary

What do all successful businesses have in common?

Whether it is HSBC bank in the city of London or a toilet cleaning business in a dusty New Delhi ghetto; they have:

- Visionary leadership
- Great people
- Good systems
- Good marketing systems
- Good business model

What is value?

Value is a quantifiable benefit both parties derive from a transaction.

What is 'Total Customer Experience'?

When a client visits your law firm, there is a certain level of service he expects from the receptionist, the lawyer and all of the administrative staff. He expects the environment to look and feel a certain way. All of those combine to form the 'total customer experience' of your firm.

- How your business will look when it is complete
- The difference or contribution your business would make to the human race
- Your lifestyle at the end of the process

How to create a vision for your law firm:

The following questions would aid you in crafting your vision:

- Why does your law firm exist?
- What difference is your firm making to your community or the world at large?
- What difference would you like your firm to make to your community or the world?
- What is the finished business going to look like ten or twenty years from the day you sat it up?
- What is your end game for your firm:
    o Are you building your firm to sell and retire?
    o Do you want to build a firm that will last far beyond you?
    o What is your end game?
- What type of employees would you want to work in your firm?
- What would your family life be five or ten years from now?
- How would you want the firm to change your life, financially, emotionally, spiritually and physically?

- What is it that you personally want to benefit from the firm?
- How much money would you need to earn to live the life you want to live five or ten years from now?

There are four stages of business growth:

- **Start-up**
- **Initial growth**
- **Momentum**
- **Breakthrough**

A system in a small to medium size law firm serves three purposes:

- It creates a framework through which every staff member will conduct their work
- It replicates the founder and gives him the freedom to work 'on' instead of 'in' the business
- It removes the chaos and uncertainty associated with most entrepreneur ventures

In order to create your own business system for your law firm, you need to answer the following questions:

- What outcome are we seeking to achieve?
- How can we measure our outcome?
- What would I need to know to achieve that outcome?
- What do I need to have to achieve that outcome?
- What results do my clients expect from me?
- What information do I need to fulfil our promise to our clients?
- What do my lawyers need to help them fulfil the firm's promise to our clients?
- What does my administrative staff need to do to fulfil our promise to our clients?
- What technologies will I need to fulfil my promise to my client?

- What additional resources would I need to fulfil my promise to my clients?

The focus of every successful business has to be:

- Customer acquisition
- Exceptional customer service provision

Chapter Two Summary

There are six specific functions of a business model

1. Articulate the value proposition – the value created to users by using the product.
2. Identify the market segment – to whom and for what purpose is the product useful; specify how revenue is generated by the firm.
3. Define the value chain – the sequence of activities and information required to allow a company to design, produce, market, deliver and support its product or service.
4. Estimate the cost structure and profit potential – using the value chain and value proposition identified.
5. Describe the position of the firm with the value network – link suppliers, customers and competitors.
6. Formulate the competitive strategy – how will you gain and hold your competitive advantage over competitors or potential new entrants.

There are three main points that needs to be covered in your marketing plan:

What is an Avatar?

It is the personality that represents who your market or your client is. It could be the key to the success of your business.

Before devising your marketing strategy you need to conduct competitive intelligence.

To conduct competitive analysis, take the following steps:

- Ask your current clients who else they currently visit for your type of service
- Conduct keyword search and find out which other firms are bidding on your keywords
- Conduct a Google search and see which businesses show up on the first few pages
- Use your Google Analytic report to see where your traffic comes from
- Use yell.com
- Use directories
- Use trade journals, look for the firms that are advertising your type of service

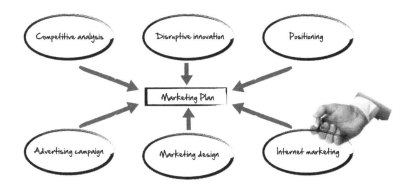

After the information gathering, the next step in the process is to analyse your competitors to know their strengths and weaknesses.

To achieve this you will need to find their:

- Marketing messages
- Offering
- Customer service provision
- Delivery mechanism

How do we get to know all of the above? Use the following tools:

First create a file on each of your main competitors. In that file you need the following information:

- Their website copies
- Their advertising material
- Their internet marketing campaigns on Google or MSM
- Their press releases
- Their services offering, past and present
- Their partners
- Their search engine and Alexa rankings
- Google alert

Also find their:

- Price point
- Accreditation
- Expertise
- Experience
- Profit margin
- Business model
- Business systems and processes
- Team competencies
- Support Material

You should also:

- Get on their mailing list
- Purchase their services
- Assess their delivery process
- Assess their customer service provision

What is disruptive innovation?

"Disruptive innovation is a process by which a product or service takes root at the bottom of a market. From there it moves up market until it displaces more established competitors. The main features of disruptive business usually include lower gross margins, smaller target markets and simpler products and services that may not appear as attractive as existing solutions when compared against traditional performance metrics".

Process of disruptive innovation

- Introduces an entirely different value proposition to the marketplace
- Initially underperforming against established products and services in the marketplace
- Product or service continuously improves until it dislodges the existing players
- It is focused more on distinction in the market place in terms of superiority of service, value, reliability, ease of use, and cost-effectiveness.

How to Effectively Position your Law Firm Above Your Competition

"The basic approach of positioning is not to create something new and different, but to manipulate what's already up there in the mind, to re-tie the connections that already exist... Positioning is an organized system for finding a window in the mind. It is based on the concept that communication can only take place at the right time and under the right circumstances".

Image selling is a very effective marketing strategy. When used properly it makes the selling process very easy. The essences of image selling are twofold:

- The image that the customer wants to portray by purchasing your service.
- The image that the customer already knows that your law firm represents.

The following steps are effective for marketing your image:

Step one – Identify the image you want to be associated with. It can either be the philosophy of the founder or the organization as a whole. It first needs to be identified along with the story of why you want to be associated with that particular image.

Step two – Communicate that image to your office designers so that it can be incorporated into the office design blueprint.

Step three – Design your work environment to reflect that image - every fixture, lighting and décor in the office needs to be congruent with that image.

Step four – Ensure all your staff members are educated on your brand image. Their uniforms, actions and interactions with customers need to reflect your projected image.

The core of advertising is to:

- take an unformulated desire, and translate it into one vivid scene of fulfilment after another.
- add the appeal of concrete satisfaction after satisfaction to the basic drive of that desire.
- make sure that your prospect realizes everything that he is getting—everything that he is now leaving behind him— everything that he may possibly be missing.

Your marketing design has to be:

- Simple
- Functional

- Clear

Chapter Three Summary

There are two pre-requisites for making 7 Figure as a lawyer:

1. Behave Like A True Professional

2. Change your Modus Operandi

"Blue Ocean" is about untapped market space, demand creation, and the opportunity for highly profitable growth".

"Red Oceans" are all of the industries currently in existence. They are the current marketplace where industry boundaries are defined and accepted, and the competitive rules of the game are well known.

Steps for creating "Blue Ocean" strategy for your law firm:

Step one – Answer the following questions:

- What factors does the legal profession take for granted, that should be eliminated?
- Which aspects should be reduced well below the legal profession's standard?
- Which factors should be raised well above the legal profession's standard?
- Which factors should be created that the legal profession has never offered?
- What are the alternative industries to the legal profession?
- Why do customers trade across the legal profession?
- What are the strategic groups in the legal profession?
- Why do clients trade up for the higher group, and why do they trade down for the lower one?
- Is there a chain of buyers in the legal profession?
- On which buyer group does the legal profession typically focus?

- If you shifted the buyer group of the legal profession, how could you unlock new value?
- What is the context in which legal service is used?
- What happens before, during, and after you provide legal services?
- Can you identify what issues keep your clients awake at night?
- How can you eliminate those problems through a complementary product or service offering?
- Does the legal profession compete on functionality or emotional appeal?
- What are the take up hurdles in rolling out a "Blue Ocean" strategy?
- By what percentage point would your "Blue Ocean" strategy increase productivity for your target market?
- If you compete on emotional appeal, what elements can you take out to make it functional?
- If you compete on functionality, what elements can be added to make it emotional?

Step two – Focus, divergence, and a compelling tagline

Focus:

When a company's value curve lacks focus, its cost structure tends to be high and its business model complex.

Divergence:

When it lacks divergence, it gets locked into a me-too strategy with no reason to stand apart in the marketplace.

Compelling tagline:

Where it lacks compelling tagline that speak to buyers, it is likely that it is internally driven or simply an example of innovation gone wrong. Commercial potential is low and it has no natural take-off capability.

Step three – Focus on:

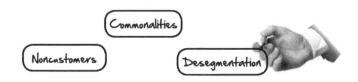

Step four – Segment your market:

Moment Of Truth is any episode in which the customer comes into contact with the organization and gets an impression of its service.

To determine the expected outcome which translates into client value, clients should be asked the following questions.

- What are your expectations for this engagement?
- What work or business do you do?
- What are your critical success factors?
- How would this engagement add value to your life?
- Which of our offerings is of the highest value to you?
- What alternatives do you have in mind presently?
- What issues are you currently confronting in relation to your business that keeps you awake at night?
- How can this engagement help you eliminate those issues?
- What standard of service do you expect from us?
- What difference would our service make to your productivity, profit, and results?
- How important is it to you for us to quickly respond to your queries?
- What would you consider to be a quick response to your queries?
- Why did you decide to change law firm?
- Why did you choose your previous law firm?
- What magazines and newspapers do you read?
- How would you define success after this engagement?

Step one – strategic pricing

Consider the following questions:

- What would it cost clients in monetary terms if they did engaged our firm?
- What in monetary value would the client gain from the engagement?
- What type of benefit would the client gain from the engagement?
- What value does the engagement bring to the client?
- How would the engagement move the client towards the achievement of his vision of the future?
- Does the engagement present any form of surprise for him?
- How much does the competition charge for a similar service?
- Has the client ever gone to another law firm?
- How much do the clients know about the service they require?
- What level of tangible or intangible value would the client get from the engagement?
- How much would the engagement cost the firm in terms of time and resources?
- What alternatives exist for your services?
- Is the client aware of the alternatives?
- How can you reposition the services in the mind of the client to make it more valuable to them?

Step two – strategic pricing

Apply the principles of price discrimination.

Step three – strategic pricing

Charge for your service according to value and not per hour.

How to create a value pricing canvas:

Step one – value pricing:

Focus on the value that you would provide to the client.

Step two – value pricing:

Focus on the cost of the service to your law firm.

Step three – value pricing:

Focus on the psychology of pricing.

Step four – value pricing:

Focus on price sensitive clients.

Step five – value pricing:

Focus on risk removal.

Step six – value pricing:

Conduct an autopsy at the end of each engagement.

Chapter Four Summary

Four principles for recruiting 'A talents':

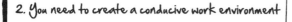

1. You should be an 'A talent' yourself (in order to sell your accounting firm to them)

2. You need to create a conducive work environment

3. You need to create good systems

4. You need to have metric for measuring staff performance

Steps for becoming an 'A talent':

Step one – Identify your talent

Step two – Identify your strength

Step three – Identify your objective

Where to find 'A talents'

- Your competition
- Events
- Your contacts
- Social media
- Recruitment Agencies
- Daily contacts
- Current employees

How to recruit 'A talents':

- 'A talent' recruitment principle 101: always be recruiting
- 'A talent' recruitment principle 102: recruit to meet a specific objective
- 'A talent' recruitment principle 103: do not settle, take as long as it is necessary to find the right candidate

Chapter Five Summary

The achievement of 'flow' requires a balance between the challenge of a task and the skill of the performer. If the task is too easy the person would experience boredom in contrary if the task is too difficult, the individual will have to raise his skill level to match the task or may not experience 'flow'.

Getting a business off the ground requires long hours of hard work, however, it does not necessarily mean that all the hard work has to be done by the entrepreneur.

Putting in long hours of hard work is not a guarantee to make a business venture successful. Success or failure has little or nothing to do with the amount of labour of love that you put in.

Key points about work-life balance:

- Successful entrepreneurship is about doing the counterintuitive
- It is not about you, it is about the mission
- You can never manage time but you can manage yourself
- Your level of performance on a given day is a function of your mental state
- 80% of what you do results in only 20% of your results

How do you ensure that as an entrepreneur lawyer you are able to create a business that serves your life?

It can be done by taking the following steps:

- List the things you do during your work day
- Arrange them in order of priority in relation to your goals
- Focus on doing the most important things first
- Eliminate the things that are not absolutely necessary to achieving your goals
- Delegate low value tasks
- Stop engaging in activities that waste the time of your employees
- Institute good systems for information dissemination within your organisation

How can you acquire the energy required to achieve your vision? Through:

Achieving work-life balance requires that you take the following steps:

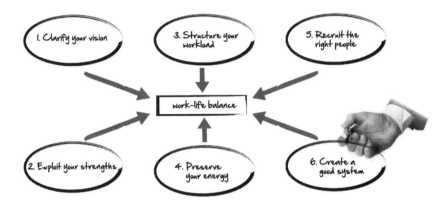

Harvard Psychologist and motivational guru David McClelland once said that change doesn't occur for one of four reasons:

- The system does not allow change
- There is no motivation to change
- We don't know what to do or how to do it
- We aren't able to do it

Transformation

No one else can change you; it is only you who can change yourself. It does not matter how many time management or work-life balance seminars you attend or books you read; if you do not make the decision to change yourself, you will not change.

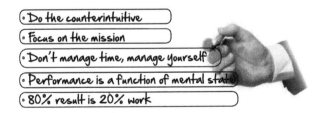

Chapter Six Summary

NLP is based on four basic principles.

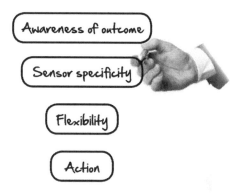

When applying the four plus one fundamentals to your business, there has to be a way in which you will be able to measure your progress.

As a business, you need to be able to conduct a gap analysis between actual and potential performance. Gap analysis answers two simple questions:

- Where are we at this moment?
- Where is our final destination?

These are the three core principles that underpin any business measurement metric:

1. Everything can be measured
2. Most measurements are subjective
3. If it cannot be measured, it has not been done right

The following are the activities you need to measure in your law firm:

- a) Marketing activities and results
- b) Customer acquisition and retention
- c) Financial performance
- d) Employee performance
- e) Business development
- f) Supplier performance
- g) Training and development

It is important that your metrics are limited to the core measurements of your business activities.

Every metric must be:

- Connected to the overall goals of your law firm
- Acceptable to all stakeholders
- Clearly measurable
- Linked to past, present and future performance of your law firm

Chapter Seven Summary

Theory of Constraint (TOC) serves two purposes. It helps in creating a framework for achieving your goals and it also serves as a diagnostic tool for identifying your core constraint.

To move your law firm from start-up to 7 Figure in twelve months using the TOC framework, you will need to go about the process as follows:

Step one – Identify your Goal. Place your goal at the top of your diagram which in this case is to make 7 Figure annually.

Step two – Identify the Critical success factor (CSF)

In this case they are five:

1. Visionary leadership or clear vision
2. Great people

3. Good system
4. Good marketing system
5. Good business model

Step three – Identify your current situation

Step four – Identify your core constraint

Chapter Eight Summary

The following are a few reasons why succession planning is absolutely imperative for a law firm:

Function

Succession planning facilitates the smooth transfer of power from one leader to the next in the events that it becomes necessary.

Identification

Senior executives, human resource, and even board members have adequate time to participate in identifying next generation leaders and talented managers who will take over departmental or key functional roles before the need arises.

Considerations

Next generation leaders are groomed and nurtured into their roles in preparation for their eventual take over when the need arises.

Benefits

Successful transition of business leaders and managers can ensure proper business continuation, minimize disruption and keep employees motivated to pursue long-term corporate objectives and business goals.

Factors to be considered in legal firm succession planning:

Effects

It is essential to take into consideration how succession planning affects the long-term future of your firm.

Essentials

Succession plans map out potential candidates to replace existing people in positions for a number of years going forward.

Need

Every organization leaders and workers will not work indefinitely. At some point, all employees retire, leave or abandon their positions for other reasons.

Internal recruitment

Succession planning encourages gegeric promotion. This encourages organization to recruit top talents that appreciate the opportunity of growing within your firm.

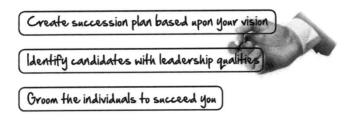

Create succession plan based upon your vision

Identify candidates with leadership qualities

Groom the individuals to succeed you

Chapter Nine Summary

Transformation of the U.S. Army from a Cold War army to one fit for the 21st century warfare came about through the implementation of the following strategies:

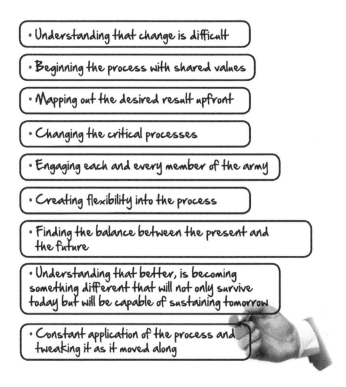

- Understanding that change is difficult
- Beginning the process with shared values
- Mapping out the desired result upfront
- Changing the critical processes
- Engaging each and every member of the army
- Creating flexibility into the process
- Finding the balance between the present and the future
- Understanding that better, is becoming something different that will not only survive today but will be capable of sustaining tomorrow
- Constant application of the process and tweaking it as it moved along

There is nothing military about these strategies. They can be implemented in your law firm.

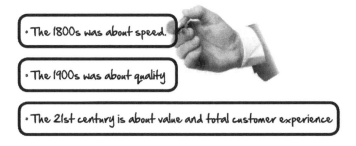

- The 1800s was about speed.
- The 1900s was about quality
- The 21st century is about value and total customer experience

Therefore, if you intend on creating a law firm that would survive the 21st century business environment, you need to ensure that you focus your service provision on those two:

- 'Total customer experience'
- Value

Chapter Ten Summary

Issues to consider in a partnership creation:

Interpersonal problems

Ensure that the individual being considered for partnership is known to the other partners on a personal basis. In business there is always the possibility of interpersonal conflict developing when the business is under stress. The business of law is a very stressful business. It is different from preparing a legal brief when the only thing at stake is your client's interest. When it is people's own money and future on the line, the reaction can be completely different. This is why it is imperative that the partners know each other on a personal basis before making the decision to get into a partnership.

Personal stability

Apart from know-how, hard work and honesty; a potential partner needs be emotionally stable. This is a very crucial point because getting into partnership with an individual who is unstable, is setting up your law firm for failure. Law firms fail because a partner decides to walk away from the partnership at a very pivotal point in the business, for personal reasons.

Integrity

Integrity is not always recognised as an aspect of business. But it is a very critical one. Business is based upon trust. Without trust, there can be no business transaction. Consequently, it is imperative that before inviting someone to become a partner in your law firm, that you either know the person personally or your background checks have cleared him.

If you do not bank on paying someone for the rest of his life to relax at a holiday resort in the Caribbean, conduct thorough background check before signing a partnership agreement. An employee you can dismiss, letting go of a partner is more complicated. You could prevent him from working in the law firm, but you will still have to continue to pay his dividend.

If a lawyer uses underhand tactics to win cases; it might bring glory to your firm. But it should also flag up your yellow alert. That's because it concerns the integrity of the person. Dishonest partners have run many businesses to the ground. So do not dismiss dishonesty as operational practice.

How to identify a good legal partner

Here is a list of steps for identifying the ideal partner for a law firm:

Step one – Find an individual who shares your values, entrepreneurial spirit and vision. This is the most important component for choosing a partner for your firm. There is going to be the need for constant communication, decision making and goal setting as you work together. Therefore, if your partner is someone who is a non-conformist, argumentative or unwilling to consider others point of view, there will be constant tension in the relationship.

Step two – Find an individual who brings diverse skills and experience to the relationship. A good business partnership should have skills that support and complement each other. No single person is good at everything. If you have great interpersonal skills but poor business finance skills; consider a partner who understands the business of law. The more skills you and your partner bring to the partnership the easier it will be to grow your firm.

Step three – Find a partner with less personal baggage. If your partner has serious challenges in his personal life, it may carry over into the business. It is nice to be willing to give someone a chance, but running a small business takes focus, time and a huge amount of energy. If your partner is dealing with one personal crisis after another you may find yourself carrying the weight of the business.

Step four – Find a partner who can offer resources and credibility to your law firm. It is great to have a law firm partner that has financial resources, but there are other contributions a partner can bring to your law firm, that are just as valuable. A partner with a strong business network, industry connections, client list, quality credentials and expertise can also increase the value of your law firm and improve your chances of achieving long term success.

Step five – Choose a partner who practices good personal and business ethics. Only enter into partnership with someone you can trust. Look for someone who values honesty, integrity and business ethics. A poorly chosen law firm partner may steal from your business, take your ideas or clients to start their own law firm or break laws that could get your law firm into trouble.

Step six – Respect is a key element of a successful partnership. You should never partner with someone who you do not respect. The main purpose of partnership formation is to achieve success as a team. You may not value the opinion and efforts of someone you do not respect at least on a professional level. You also want to partner with someone who will show you respect as a partner, business professional and as the founder of your business.

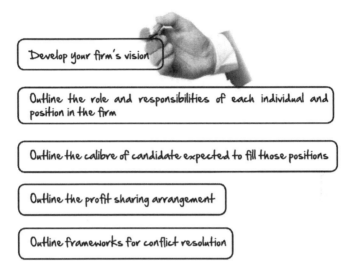

Develop your firm's vision

Outline the role and responsibilities of each individual and position in the firm

Outline the calibre of candidate expected to fill those positions

Outline the profit sharing arrangement

Outline frameworks for conflict resolution

Appendix

- Advantages and Disadvantages of New Technology | eHow.com. Available http://www.ehow.com/info_8112855_advantages-disadvantages-new-technology.html#ixzz1iwyzxQGo. Accessed on 3dr May 2012.
- Albrecht, K. 2002. The Only Thing That Matters: Bringing the Power of the Customer into the Center of Your Business. Harper Business. New York.
- Albrecht, K. 1994. The Northbound Train: Finding the Purpose, Setting the Direction, Shaping the Destiny of Your Organization. American Management Association. New York.
- Art of war. Available http://www.marketing-intelligence.co.uk/resources/competitor-analysis.htm. Accessed on 3dr May 2012.
- August, J. and Koltin, A. D. "How to Lose Clients without Really Trying." Journal of Accountancy, May 1992: 67–70.
- Aur-um. Available http://www.aur-um.com.ua/eng/?gclid=COOV7qvJwq0CFUWH4godbk98AQ. Accessed on 3dr May 2012.
- Bergstrand, J. 2009. Reinvent Your Enterprise: Through Better Knowledge Work. Brand Velocity Atlanta.
- Berry, Leonard L. and Seltman, D. K. 2008. Management Lessons from the Mayo Clinic: Inside One of the World's Most Admired Service Organizations. McGraw-Hill. New York.
- Bosworth, M. T. 1994. Solution Selling: Creating Buyers in Difficult Selling Markets. Irwin Professional Publishing. Chicago.
- Bosworth, M T. and Holland J. 2004. Customer Centric Selling. McGraw-Hill. New York.
- Boress, A. 1994. The "I Hate Selling" Book. AMACOM. New York.
- Bransford, J. Brown, A and Cocking, R. 1999. How People Learn: Brain, Mind, Experience, and School. Library of Congress in Publication.

- Breyfogle, F. 2008. Improvement Project Execution: A Management and Black Belt Guide for Going. Bridgeway Books.
- Business model. Available http://www.audiencedialogue.net/busmod.html. Accessed on 3dr May 2012.
- Business model. Available http://hbr.org/2002/05/why-business-models-matter/ar/1. Accessed on 3dr May 2012.
- Business model. Available http://www.in2in.org/insights/Pourdehnad-IdealizedDesign.pdf. Accessed on 3dr May 2012.
- Chesbrough, H. and Rosenbloom, R. 2003 Business Model. Available http://www.cfses.com/documents/pharma/32-Business_Models_Rasmussen.pdf. Accessed on 3dr May 2012.
- Collins, J. 2001. Good to Great. Harper Business.
- Collins, J. and Porras, J. 2002. Built to Last. Harper Business essentials.
- Cram, T. 2006. Smarter Pricing: How to Capture More Value in Your Market. Prentice Hall. London.
- David A. 2000. Learning in Action: A Guide to Putting the Learning Organization to Work. Harvard Business School Press. Boston.
- Dawson, R. 2005. Developing Knowledge-Based Client Relationships: The Future of Professional Services. Butterworth Heinemann. Boston.
- Doctorsofusc. Available http://www.doctorsofusc.com/services/health-tips/brain-tumors. Accessed on 3dr May 2012.
- Donald, E. 1995. Esq. How Lawyers Screw Their Clients and What You Can Do About It. Barricade Books, Inc. New York.
- Drukker, P. Available http://commnerd.wordpress.com/2008/02/21/the-aim-of-marketing-peter-drucker/. Accessed on 3dr May 2012.
- Drukker, P. 1954. The Practice of Management. Harper Business Essential.
- Drukker, P. and Walsh, J. quotes. Available http://results.com/book-summaries/topgrading-how-leading-companies-win-by-hiring-coaching-and-keeping-the-best-people-bradford-d-smart. Accessed on 3dr May 2012.

- E. Andrew Boyd. 2007. The Future of Pricing: How Airline Ticket Pricing Has Inspired a Revolution. Palgrave Macmillan. New York.
- eHow.com. How to Manage the Costs of New Technology. Available http://www.ehow.com/how_7994731_manage-costs-new-technology.html#ixzz1iwzOneCI. Accessed on 3dr May 2012.
- Ferguson, M. 1987. The Aquarian Conspiracy. St. Martins Press. New York.
- Florida, R. 2007. The Flight of the Creative Class: The New Global Competition for Talent. HarperBusiness. New York.
- Florida, Richard. 2004 The Rise of the Creative Class: And How It's Transforming Work, Leisure, Community and Everyday Life. Basic Books. New York.
- Flow. Available http://en.wikipedia.org/wiki/Mihaly_Csikszentmihalyi. Accessed on 3dr May 2012.
- Ford, H. 1927. "I will build a car for the great multitude". Available http://www.troynovant.com/Franson-WR/Ford/Model-T-Ford.html. Accessed on 3dr May 2012.
- Frederick, F. and Thomas, T. 1996. The Loyalty Effect: The Hidden Force Behind Growth, Profits, and Lasting Value. Harvard Business School Press. Boston.
- Gardiner, H. 2010 More Doctors Giving Up Private Practices. Available http://www.nytimes.com/2010/03/26/health/policy/26docs.html?pagewanted=all. Accessed on 3dr May 2012.
- Gates, B. Available http://inventors.about.com/od/inventormagazines/tp/bill_gates.htm. Accessed on 3dr May 2012.
- Gates, B. 1992. Take our best 20 people away. Available http://blogs.hbr.org/cs/2011/12/what_it_takes_to_win_extreme_1.html. Accessed on 3dr May 2012.
- Gates, B. 1996. The Road Ahead. Penguin Books.
- Gilad, B. Why we need competitive intelligent. Available http://mysite.verizon.net/vzesz4a6/current/id1230.html. Accessed on 3dr May 2012.
- Golden, M. 2010. Social Media Strategies for Professionals and their Firms: The Guide to Establishing Credibility and

Accelerating Relationships. John Wiley Sons, Inc. Hoboken, NJ.

- Goleman, D. 2011. The Power of Emotional Intelligence. More Than Sound LLC.
- Gordon, R. and Harper, M. 1996. Hope Is Not a Method: What Business Leaders Can Learn from America's Army. Broadway Books. New York.
- Gregory, J. M. 1995. The Seven Laws of Teaching. Grand Rapids. MI: Baker Books.
- Harrington, J. 1991. Business Process Improvement: The Breakthrough Strategy for Total Quality. The Library of Congress in Publication.
- Hope navigators. Available http://www.hopenavigators.com/tipping-the-scales/cutting-edge-technology. Accessed on 3dr May 2012.
- Hopkins, C. Scientific Marketing. Available at: ReallySimpleMedia.com. Accessed on 3dr May 2012.
- James, B. and Swartz, J. 2006. Seeing David in the Stone: Find and Seize Great Opportunities Using 12 Actions Mastered by 70 Highly Successful Leaders. Carmel, IN: Leading Books Press.
- Jobs, S.1993. "Do you want to sell sugar water for the rest of your life, or do you want to come with me and change the world?" Available http://37signals.com/svn/posts/2813-do-youwant-to-sell-sugar-water-for. Accessed on 3dr May 2012.
- Kent, B. Pricing. 2003. Making Profitable Decisions, 3rd ed. McGraw-Hill. New York.
- Kim, W. C. and Mauborgne, R. 2005. Blue Ocean Strategy. Harvey Business School Publication.
- Kirkpatrick, D. and Kirkpatrick, J. 2006. Evaluating Training Programs: The Four Levels. Barrett-Koehler Publisher.
- Laura, E. 2007. Managing the Modern Law Firm: New Challenges, New Perspectives. Oxford University Press. Oxford, UK.
- LeBoeuf, M. 2000. How to Win Customers and Keep Them for Life: Revised and Updated for the Digital Age. Berkley Books. New York.
- Magretta, J. May 2002. Models Matter. Harvard Business Review.

- Maister, D. 1997. True Professional. Simon & Schuster.
- Market demand and value. Available http://www.worldscibooks.com/etextbook/7171/7171_chap07.pdf. Accessed on 3dr May 2012.
- Maxwell, S. PhD. 2008. The Price Is Wrong: Understanding What Makes a Price Seem Fair and the True Cost of Unfair Pricing. John Wiley & Sons, Inc. Hoboken, NJ.
- McCumber D. 2011. Buying Craze: Hospital Groups Acquiring Physicians' Private Practices. Available http://mccumberdaniels.wordpress.com/2011/04/18/buying-crazehospital-groups-acquiring-physicians%E2%80%99-private-practices/. Accessed on 3dr May 2012.
- Mohammed, R. 2005. The Art of Pricing: How to Find the Hidden Profits to Grow Your Business. Crown Business. New York.
- Mohammed, R. 2010. The 1% Windfall: How Successful Companies Use Price to Profit and Grow. Harper Business. New York.
- Mohammed, R. 2005. The Art of Pricing: How to Find the Hidden Profits to Grow Your Business. Crown Business. New York.
- Mourkogiannis, N. 2006. Purpose: The Starting Point of Great Companies. Palgrave Macmillan. New York.
- NLP. Available http://nlpanchoringexplained.com/what-is-nlp/. Accessed on 3dr May 2012.
- Ogilvy, D.1985. Advertising. Vintage Books. New York.
- Peakdocs. Available http://www.peakdocs.com/NewsUpdates/reviews.html. Accessed on 3dr May 2012.
- Peter, F. 1995. Managing in a Time of Great Change. Truman Talley Books/Dutton. New York.
- Peter F. 1993. The Effective Executive. Harper Business. New York.
- Pettengill, S. 1930. The successful producer of an article. Available http://www.boardofwisdom.com/mailquote.asp?msgid=13140. Accessed on 3dr May 2012.

- Prlog. Available http://www.prlog.org/11221928-take-look-into-medical-training-for-2011-with-cutting-edge-technology-at-empire-medical-training.html. Accessed on 3dr May 2012.
- Reis, A. and Trout, J. 2001. Positioning. US. The McGrew-Hill Companies, Inc.
- Richard, B. 2008. Why Popcorn Costs So Much at the Movies: And Other Pricing Puzzles. Copernicus Books. New York.
- Richard, C. E. 1989. Beyond The Billable Hour: An Anthology of Alternative Billing Methods. American Bar Association. Chicago.
- Richard, C. E. 1992. Win-Win Billing Strategies: Alternatives That Satisfy Your Clients and You. American Bar Association. Chicago.
- Richard, E. 2008. The End of Lawyers?: Rethinking the Nature of Legal Services. Oxford University Press. New York.
- Richard, H. and Sunstein, C. 2008. Nudge: Improving Decisions About Health, Wealth, and Happiness. Yale University Press. New Haven, CT.
- Roman God. Available http://iic.wiki.fgv.br/file/view/the+ambidextrous+organization.pdf. Accessed on 3dr May 2012.
- Ronald, J. 2006. Pricing on Purpose: Creating and Capturing Value. John Wiley & Sons, Inc. Hoboken, NJ.
- Ronald, J. and Paul D. 2003. The Firm of the Future: A Guide for Accountants, Lawyers, and Other Professional Services. John Wiley & Sons, Inc. Hoboken, NJ.
- Semler, R. 2003. The Seven-Day Weekend: A Better Way to Work in the 21st Century. Arrow Books. London.
- Seth, G. 2002. Purple Cow: Transform Your Business by Being Remarkable. New York: Portfolio.
- Slywotzky, A. 1996, Value Migration. Library of Congress in Publication Data.
- Smart, B. 1999. Top Grading. Penguin Group.
- Smith, A. 1993. An Inquiry into the Nature and Causes of the Wealth of Nations. Regnery Publishing, Inc. Washington, DC.
- Stawicki, E. 2011Independent medical practices find it harder to stay that way. Available

http://minnesota.publicradio.org/display/web/2011/05/14/independent-medical-practice/. Accessed on 3dr May 2012.

- Steven, E. 1996. Price Theory and Applications, 3rd ed. West Publishing. St. Paul, MN.

- Sveiby, K. 1997. The New Organizational Wealth: Managing and Measuring Knowledge-Based Assets. Berrett-Koehler Publishers, Inc. San Francisco, CA.

- The Advantages of New Technology in Business | eHow.com. Available http://www.ehow.com/list_7499096_advantages-new-technology-business.html#ixzz1iwyn4gjF. Accessed on 3dr May 2012.

- The profit experts. Available http://theprofitexperts.co.uk/Doctors/archives/how-to-acquire-the-latest-cutting-edge-medical-technology. Accessed on 3dr May 2012.

- Thomas, H. 2005. Thinking for a Living: How to Get Better Performance and Results from Knowledge Workers. Harvard Business School Press. Boston.

- Walter, M. 1992. The Deming Management Method. Gold Arrow Publication.

- Weiss, A. 2008. Value-Based Fees: How to Charge—and Get—What You're Worth. Jossey-Bass/Pfeiffer. San Francisco.

- Williams, T. 2010. Positioning for Professionals: How Professional Knowledge Firms Can Differentiate Their Way to Success. John Wiley & Sons, Inc. Hoboken, NJ.

- William, J. E. 1995. Marketing for CPAs, Accountants, and Tax Professionals. Haworth Press. New York.

- Wootton, D. 2006. Bad Medicine: Doctors Doing Harm Since Hippocrates. Oxford University Press. New York.

Great Books by Romeo

As sold on... amazon.com

Book Romeo now! +44(0)78 650 49508

27.9% The Most Effective Retail Shrinkage Reduction Technologies

Prior to investing in any technology, there are vital questions that need to answered; those questions along with their answers can be found in this e-book.

This e-book was conceived out of our own desperate efforts to answer those questions.

What you will learn:

- Technologies That Prevent Employee Theft
- Technologies That Prevent Shoplifting

- Receiving Technologies
- Multi-purpose Technologies

12.24% The Most Effective Retail Employee Error Reduction Strategies

Employee errors in pricing, accounting and receiving contribute approximately 18% of retail shrinkage; this equates to £18,623 in losses to an average supermarket or store and almost £49,679 in losses to a superstore. This means that a store or supermarket that operates with a 1% net profit will need to make an additional £3million in annual sales in order to recover profit lost due to employee errors. By the same measure a typical hyper store will need to increase its sales by £8million.

You will learn:

- Constitutes as Retail Employee Error
- to Calculate the Cost of Employee Error
- to Calculate Additional Sales Required to Recover Losses Caused by Employee Error
- of Employee Error
- to Reduce Employee Error
- Ultimate Employee Error Prevention Formula
- to Apply the Lessons from This E-Book to Your Business

43.5% The Most Effective Retail Profit Protection Strategies

The retail landscape is changing rapidly with the constant increase in internet shopping. From 2005 to 2009, the online shopping population grew to 1.6 billion.

It is predicted to rise to 2.3 billion by 2014 with gross revenue totalling $778.6 billion. This is bad news for traditional brick and mortar retail businesses.

The question is: are you prepared? You will find your answer in this eBook.

What you will learn:

- The Conventional Approach to Loss prevention
- Why Loss Prevention is Critical to Retail
- Loss Prevention Spending vs Return on Investment
- What You Are Losing
- Profit vs Sales Calculation
- How to Create a Culture of Loss Prevention
- Effective Shrinkage Management Strategies
- The Ultimate Profit Protection Formula

24.5% The Most Effective Perishable And Non-Perishable Shrinkage Reduction Strategies

This e-book is jam packed with information on the causes of retail shrinkage, types of retail shrinkage, the cost of shrinkage to the retail industry and how shrinkage can be prevented. It is a comprehensive e-book on how and why shrinkage occurs and it provides a step-by-step guide on how to prevent shrinkage.

You will learn:

- An Introduction to Perishable Shrinkage
- Breakdown of Perishable Shrinkage
- Causes of Perishable Shrinkage
- How to Prevent Perishable Shrinkage
- The Ultimate Perishable Shrinkage Prevention Formula
- An Introduction to Non-Perishable Shrinkage
- Classification of Non-Perishable Shrinkage
- Breakdown of Non-Perishable Shrinkage
- Strategies for Preventing Non-Perishable Shrinkage
- The Ultimate Non-Perishable Shrinkage Prevention Formula
- How to Apply The Lessons From This E-Book to Your Business

27.8% The Most Effective Retail Employee Theft Reduction Strategies

The majority of retail employees are decent people who go to work each day to serve their customers and make their living.

However, there are the rotten apples that contaminate the good names of the rest.

This e-book is an instructional guide to retailers to show them how to minimise and prevent employee theft in their stores. Like shoplifting most incidents of employee theft occur because the opportunity exists. When retailers remove the opportunity, they can reduce the possibilities. This e-book will show retailers how to remove the opportunities that allow employee theft in their stores.

You will learn:

- Why Employees Steal
- The Process of Employee Theft
- Signs of Employee Theft
- How to Calculate the Cost of Employee Theft
- How to Prevent Employee Theft
- How Technology Can Help Prevent Employee Theft
- The Ultimate Employee Theft Prevention Formula

84%: The Most Effective Strategies for Increasing Retail Profit

The formula for increasing profit in retail is to increase sales and reduce shrinkage. How can retailers increase sales and reduce shrinkage? The answer is in this book.

You will learn everything you need to know about:

- Creating a Culture of Loss Prevention
- Employee Error
- Employee Theft
- Shoplifting
- Perishable and Non-Perishable Shrinkage
- Receiving Shrinkage
- Technologies that Help to Reduce Retail Shrinkage

Soon to be Published Books by Romeo

Book Romeo now! +44(0)78 650 49508

Visual Merchandise: How to Create a Beautiful Yet Profitable Display

Merchandise display is the most effective form of advertising for a retail store. The more attractive a display, the higher the possibility of increasing sales. This book will show retailers how to create a display that is so attractive that it would increase their footfall tenfold.

You will learn:

- The psychology behind visual merchandising
- How to use visual merchandising to increase retail sales
- Challenges facing visual merchandisers
- How to burst the price myth with creative merchandise display
- The best merchandise display strategies
- How to maximise display space allocation with creative fixtures
- The pros and cons of using a planogram
- The pros and cons of hiring visual merchandising companies
- Most effective visual merchandise technologies
- How to display merchandise for maximum profit

Store Design Blueprint: How to Design an Attractive But Profitable Store

There are three fundamental principles that underpin a retail store design:

1. Attract customers as they pass by the store
2. Entice them to enter the store
3. Persuade them to buy

The aim of this book is to show retailers how to apply these principles to this store design.

You will learn:

- Store design psychology – what you must know to succeed
- Store design – Image selling
- How to use store design to increase sales
- Store design for increased customer flow
- Choosing your store colour and layout
- The best retail store lighting system
- How to wow customers with creative storefront design
- How to choose the right materials for store design
- Designing store for profit – design security
- Store design technologies

How to Market and Manage A Professional Firm Series: How to make 7 Figure annually as a doctor, dentist, accountant, lawyer, consultant and private security firm owner.

There are four elements essential for the success of any business:

1. Visionary leadership
2. Great people
3. Good system
4. Good marketing system

In the How to Market and Manage A Professional Firm Series, we teach professional entrepreneurs how to effectively utilize these four elements for the development of their businesses.

Many professionals are good technicians. They are good at their professions, however, when it comes to running business they are challenged.

The aim of the 7 Figure Code Books Series is to show professionals how to enhance their technical skills and apply similar levels of structural thinking into building a 7 Figure business.

There is no reason why a doctor or lawyer should not be able to easily make 7 Figure per annum. We show them how to achieve this in the How to Market and Manage A Professional Firm Series.

You will learn:

- How to create an effective business system that runs on auto-pilot
- How to recruit and retain only top talents
- How to develop an effective marketing system
- How to create new market for a product or service
- How the attract new clients and retain existing ones

Book Romeo

Book Romeo now by calling:
+44(0)78 650 49508

Or email: romeo@theprofitexperts.co.uk

Printed in Great Britain
by Amazon